brain magic

*HOW TO HYPNOTIZE COWORKERS
TO DO YOUR LAUNDRY!*

darren mark michalczuk

Brain Magic

Copyright © 2017 by Darren Mark Michalczuk

No part of this publication may be reproduced, distributed, or transmitted in any form or by any means, including photocopying, recording, or other electronic or mechanical methods, without the prior written permission of the author, except in the case of brief quotations embodied in critical reviews and certain other non-commercial uses permitted by copyright law.

Tellwell Talent

www.tellwell.ca

ISBN

978-1-77370-089-2 (Paperback)

table of contents

Preface vii

My Brain Is Faster Than Your Brain. 1

To Get Faster, You'll Have To Change Your Mind. 7

What A Great Story. 13

Imagine That. 19

Directions 27

You Can Set A Memory Alarm. 31

I've Experienced The 'Butterfly Effect'. 37

Your Mind Is A Palace. 43
  Kids Palace   49

Movies. 53
  The Teens   58

Household Items 61

The Rest Of 'My Mind'. 65
  Mega Palace   67
  Store Palace   71

Camp Palace   75

Car Palace   79

School Palace   83

Farm Palace   87

House Palace   91

Sports Palace   95

Beach Palace   99

Body Palace   103

Imagine The Possibilities. 107

Birthdays. 113

You've Got The Whole World In Your Hands. 117

Take A Number. 121

Phone Numbers. 129

Go Ahead. Make Some Memories. I Dare You. 133

I Offer A Thousand Pardons. 139

I Have A Special Card For You. 145

A Word Is Worth A Thousand Pictures. 155

Spelling Says A Lot About Hoo You Are.. 159

What's In A Name?. 169

Names. 179

Name Game. 185

Zookeeper 189

There Will Be Blank Pages.. 195

Map Maker 201

Imagine Me, Like One Of Your French Words. 205

Learn To Take Notes. 211

I've Hidden One More Memory Secret. 221

The Twelfth Poster 227

Logo Designs 233

It's Not Cheating. Honest. 239

With Great Power Comes Great… Um… Greatness. 245

I Feel Numb From Numbers. 251

I Felt Like I Was Raised By Wolves. 261

I Bet I'm Less Competitive Than You. 267

Brain Magic Trivia 273

More Memory Challenges 277

Biography 279

preface

When I was in high school I really had no idea what I was going to do in life. Actually, I still don't, but that's not the point. I had teachers who tried to guide me into fields other than education such as engineering, probably because my marks showed my skills in other areas. My math percentage marks in grades 10, 11, and 12 were 94, 95, and 96 respectively. In 1990, after high school, I registered at Grant MacEwan College believing I was taking 'pre-med' courses to someday work as a doctor when I really couldn't stand the sight of blood or mucus. In actuality I was taking science courses that could be applied to an education degree, which apparently was my destiny. Deep down I guess I really wanted to eventually work in a school teaching my nieces and nephew. I also loved the smell of art paste and Lysol.

I didn't really find a lot of value in the courses I took, but I knew I had to finish my degree in education if I wanted to sit behind the coveted 1960s-style giant wooden desk. I sat through Art History 101 learning about architectural styles and designs of Catholic churches, prestigious schools, and banquet halls knowing full well that I would someday be teaching 'clay sculpturing' to elementary students. I only hoped that my little prodigies wouldn't eat the brightly-coloured art clay.

After spending a few days at my practicum school where I would be spending a few weeks observing in the classroom as part of my training, I noticed something that changed how I looked at education. Most of the kids in the class couldn't do even the most basic skills. In math, for example, they couldn't add or multiply without counting fingers or drawing lines on the pages. Some couldn't add or multiply at all, and yet they were learning concepts that needed these skills. Kids who couldn't do 6 x 7 were asked to find the area of a rectangle with a width of 6 and a length of 7.

At first I thought this was just a weak class, but through my 20 years plus of teaching math I realized that this lack of knowledge is everywhere. Each year some classes are stronger than others, but the numbers are almost always the same. Some kids get it, some kids struggle, and some kids are completely lost. Those who can master the basic skills, whether it is music, math, or language, generally perform well in these classes. The more than two thirds who haven't mastered the basics generally struggle or find ways to pretend they aren't. Teachers have even come up with ways to make it seem like their students are succeeding.

While watching late night television one night I saw an ad for a memory program. A few weeks later I bought this program from the 'As Seen on TV' store at the mall. That's when I became interested in memory. I didn't actually use any of the skills that were taught in this program because I knew that images like a six shooter and cigarettes wouldn't work well with children; however, I did become interested in advanced learning techniques. I started experimenting with using memory skills to teach the times tables.

Over the next few years I developed specific ways of teaching not only numbers in math, but notes in music and letters in language arts. I found that teaching kids how to memorize information they would be using on a daily basis allowed me to spend time that would normally be spent on practice worksheets on other things like performing plays, building wood projects, and writing 'choose your own adventure' stories. Essentially, memorizing changed everything in class.

Though the years, however, there has always been resistance. There have been parents doubting this 'out-of-the-box' thinking, administration wanting me to stick to the 1960s *Guidelines for Learning* textbook, and YouTube trolls who want to mock anything they don't understand. There have always been people who will resist change like it's the Confederate Army. (Sorry, that analogy sounded cooler in my head.) I have had my job threatened so many times that I feel as though I've been playing the bumbling neighbour on an 80s sitcom for twelve seasons. But all this has been worth it when I think of how many children I've taught who have gone from hating to loving school.

My brain is faster than your brain.

(Some can memorize a full deck of cards, while others can't remember the cards in their hands.)

After practicing for one week an eight-year-old girl learned to memorize the order of a shuffled deck in minutes.

Q: *Which word makes the sentence above amazing? Without this word, it would just be interesting. It is a very important word that represents what this book is about.*

I read somewhere that in the Olympics they should have one competitor who is an average athlete so that spectators could see how truly exceptional the other athletes are. In the sprint races we would see the winners crossing the line while 'Average Joe' was still at the halfway point of the track. Shot-putters would look like they had thrown a home run while the 'off-the-street' athlete barely got it out of the infield. Swimmers would appear to be driving a speedboat while the 'token swimmer' was paddling a canoe.

This would really put the Olympic Games into perspective, as it would give spectators a benchmark to measure athleticism. It would give new meaning to the numbers that mark distances or times. Even those who weren't medal winners would seem to have superhuman strength compared to those who didn't train or qualify. Many people would look at the Olympics in a different light.

We could do the same for kids in school. To make this easy and measurable, let's start by taking a look at math. In any given math class you will have students like Sarah, Carmen, and Marcie repeatedly doing simple calculations such as adding and multiplying. Even when they do other tasks such as long multiplication and division, they are essentially using these basic facts over and over. No matter what strand of mathematics they are doing, basically they are answering questions such as '7+5' or '8×9'.

Now these three girls make these calculations at different speeds. Sarah, whose mom is a schoolteacher, is able to answer each question quickly. She has practiced by using flashcards that her dad gives her on car rides and she has worked through many puzzle books containing these types of questions. Her average speed for answering each basic multiplication question is one per second.

Carmen isn't as fast. She has to count on her fingers or draw tally lines to come up with most of the answers. She uses the finger trick that her teacher taught her to use with the nine times table. She is ok with counting by fives. By the time she comes up with an answer to a word problem, most of the other students have usually moved on to the next problem. On average she can answer each multiplication question in about 10 seconds.

Marcy struggles in math. She can answer simple multiplication questions like 2×3 or 4×5, but for any question that the answer is higher than 20, she almost always gets it wrong. She often copies from another student's work.

Although she won't get every answer correct, if she is given enough time to come up with an answer, on average she could answer each multiplication question in approximately 45 seconds or even longer.

To actually see how big of a difference this variation makes, we could compare these three students as if they were drivers in a city. Let's say Carmen would be able to drive through the city at 10 km/h. She would need to stop at every traffic signal or sign, taking the time to slowly read and figure each one out. She would also have to stop often to ask for directions, but would still end up at the wrong location at times. Comparatively, Sarah would be able to drive safely through the same city at 100 km/h, taking all the shortcuts on roads where it is legal to drive this fast. She would always arrive at where she was going well before anyone else, every single time.

This would also mean that Marcy would only be able to drive as fast as she could walk. She would not understand the traffic signals or signs and she would turn left instead of right, drive through red lights, stop at green ones, and blindly go through railway crossings being lost all the while.

When we actually focus on the numbers that measure skills, it is easy to see how far apart students are in terms of ability. Within one class some students answer questions as if they are driving a Ferrari, others answer questions as if they are driving a moped with a flat tire, and still others answer questions as if they are waiting for a bus on some random street. These skills vary not only in math, but also in other subject areas like language or music.

Now here's a quick test for you to check your memory ability. Give yourself 60 seconds to memorize the following list of words. Remember, each word has to be in the correct order when you write it down. You get one point for each word you spell correctly in the right order. Go ahead and set your phone timer for one minute. Study these words for 60 seconds, and then close this page. Try to write down as many words as you can remember in the right order.

1. gravity
2. health
3. wrist
4. pylon
5. radar
6. anxious
7. soccer
8. notebook
9. bitter
10. faith
11. elevate
12. cactus
13. conflict
14. pirate
15. feather
16. baby
17. sweet
18. bold
19. sparkle
20. stream

Now, just to put things into perspective, most people get between four and seven words correct. However, with training and practice, it is possible to remember a list of 20 words in less than 30 seconds and a list of 100 words in less than five minutes.

To find a solution to getting all of the students doing schoolwork as if they are driving a Ferrari, we have to take a look at some "exceptional" people. These people have abilities that go beyond anyone in their homeroom class. They have abilities that are greater than anyone else in their school. In fact they have abilities that are beyond anyone in their hometown, including the adults.

These people can memorize a list of 100 random words in less than five minutes when most people can only memorize four or five. This means that if the average person can lift 50 pounds, these people can lift 1000 pounds. They can also memorize this list even when it is presented in a scrambled order (such as the 87th word being placed first, for example).

These same people can memorize a deck of cards in just a few minutes. While most people can barely remember three or four cards in order, these people can remember at least ten times more. It really is remarkable when we consider memory in this comparative way. Imagine making ten times more money than you do right now, or being able to do ten times more errands in a day, or having ten times more children in your house. I guess if you don't have any children in your house then this won't really change things, but you get the idea.

These children can memorize hundreds of names and faces of people they have never met, long lists of random numbers, numerous dates of events that are actual or fictional, or connections between abstract images. Essentially anything that can be put into measurable information, they can memorize, and they can do it quickly.

Now what is really amazing about these people is that they are just regular people with incredible skills, some of them as young as ten years old. This is something that anyone can do. Yep, anyone.

to get faster, you'll have to change your mind.

(I'll race you home, but I know a few shortcuts.)

Some people say mnemonics are just simple tricks…and they are right.

I once offered a memory workshop in a larger city for a literacy convention. I invited a parent of one of the students in my class to come along and he sat at the back of the room while I did my presentation. He later reported to me that one woman in the audience had been whispering to people beside her that I was teaching nothing more than "parlour tricks". At first when I heard this, I laughed, mostly to hide my own personal insecurities. After I had thought about it, however, I realized she was right. These were just simple tricks, things anyone could learn in a short amount of time. Awesome.

Imagine being ten years old and racing your best friend to his house. You know the way, but he knows a shortcut. He wins by at least ten minutes, which is even more frustrating considering it only took him two minutes to get home. If this keeps happening every day, it would be frustrating to never find the shortcut. You see him duck into an opening through some trees, but you can't seem to find the path he takes. In classrooms, this is what is happening. Some students know a shortcut - a way to remember how to multiply numbers, read words, or play notes - and this advantage allows them to be faster than the other kids. Most times they don't even realize they think differently.

We all have these shortcuts or at least know some of them. Most of us have learned the name 'ROY G BIV' to remember the colours of the rainbow (Red, Orange, Yellow, Green, Blue, Indigo, and Violet). Some know the word 'HOMES' to remember the Great Lakes (Lake **H**uron, Lake **O**ntario, Lake **M**ichigan, Lake **E**rie, and Lake **S**uperior). In music class, some of us have learned the phrase '**E**very **G**ood **B**oy **D**eserves **F**udge' to remember the notes on the lines of a staff of music, which beginning from the bottom are E G B D F.

These strategies don't have to be complicated. Parents of larger families have a way of remembering their children's names, usually by birth order starting with the oldest. A mother can remember what she needs to buy at the grocery store by visualizing the fridge. A student in math class can remember what five times seven is by counting up by fives. Whether we do it on purpose or not, these are considered mnemonics or ways to remember something.

Some mnemonics are more effective than others. For example, my grade four teacher taught me to spell 'turtle' by having me remember the sentence: '**T**hey **U**se **R**ocks **T**o **L**ay **E**ggs.' Now, I liked my teacher and she was doing the best she could, but she was essentially asking me to remember six letters by having me memorize 21 letters. This was not an effective strategy, but she tried. Once we start seeing that there are other ways to remember, we can start choosing the ways that are faster and more effective.

In music class, many teachers will use a 'circle of fifths' diagram to remember how many sharps are in a song. Now I know what you are thinking. This is going to be boring. You're right. It is boring. Even the name is painful. Bear with me though, because I probably have a point.

This is a way to teach kids how many sharps (or flats) are in a song with a certain key. For example, a song in the key of A has three sharps. On a piano, these notes are basically the next key up from a white key (usually black). The music term for this is a 'half step' higher. A song can have anywhere from zero to seven sharps. Learning how many sharps there are in songs with different keys is an important part of music.

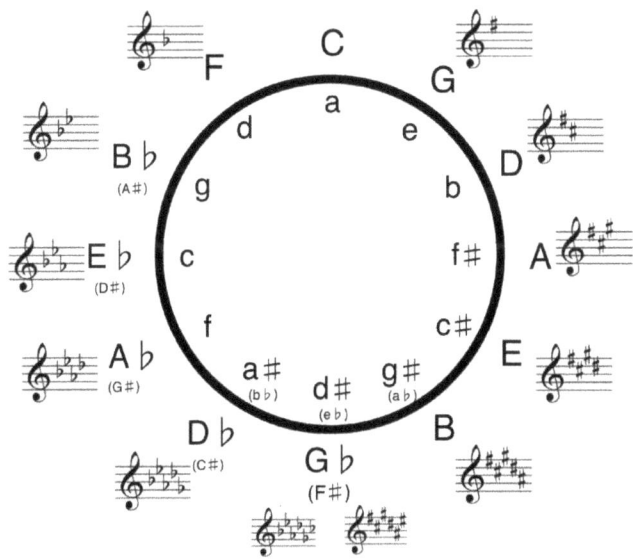

Now when you see this diagram you will see how much information a student will have to decode in order to come up with the number of sharps or flats in a song. They will have to memorize, or at least see, the pattern of letters that go around the circle, find the letter of the key signature they are in, and then count to find the number of sharps for a song. For me, I didn't really find this way of learning about sharps worked.

Although I learned music when I was younger, I relearned how to read and play music as an adult after I had studied mnemonics. I created a way to remember these same musical concepts and used this to teach my students. I used the capital letter of each key as a way to remember how many sharps were in a song. For example, to remember that in the key of 'A' there are three sharps, I remembered that the letter 'A' has three sharp corners since it's shaped like a triangle. To know how many sharps were in a song all I had to do was look at how many sharp corners the (key) letter had. This was a little easier for my students and me to understand.

The other letters follow this same pattern. The letter 'C' is shaped like an 'O' and this tells me that the key of C has no sharps. The letter 'E', which is basically a square shape with four corners, tells me that the key of E has four sharps, just like a square has four sharp corners. Now when I ask one of my ten-year-old students, "How many sharps are in the key of A?" or "Which key has no sharps?" the answers come lightning fast.

This specific technique of remembering a tough concept in music is something that took some work. People who work in a specific area will often find a way to remember important items in a similar way. A friend of mine who was a First Aid instructor for years came up with a way to remember the vital signs. Vital signs are the signs of life that should be checked by a trained responder (such as a paramedic). He remembered five vital signs using an image of a person's upper body.

This instructor would start at the top of the head, which he used to remember the level of consciousness or how alert the person was. Next is the forehead, which he used to remember the skin colour, temperature, and moisture. Below the forehead are the eyes, which are checked for equality, reaction, and size. Under the eyes are the mouth and nose to help remember breathing, which is checked for rate, depth, and regularity. Finally, below this is the heart, which is also checked for rate, strength, and regularity.

When he was going to help someone, either in a simulated scene for practice or in a real life situation, he had cues that helped him to remember these important items. Sometimes the stress of a situation will make it hard to remember even the simplest things, but he could always find these 'memory landmarks' to help him check and treat an injured person.

Now back to the original question: What is the most important word in this sentence? The answer is 'learned'.

> After practicing for one week an eight-year-old girl <u>learned</u> to memorize the order of a shuffled deck in minutes.

"Learned" is an incredibly important word as it shows that memorizing is something that anyone can do instead of being an ability that you are born with. People who can remember much more than the average person can create memory devices at will and for almost any purpose. In seconds they can create a way to remember information. Though this does take practice and it doesn't happen by accident, anyone can learn to do it.

What a great story.

(I remember a story I haven't read since I was a child, but I can't remember that computer symbol I see every day.)

Which do you remember more from elementary school: math worksheets, or funny stories about your friends?

If we are going to be able to remember things in the manner of a 'genius', then we have to understand how the mind works. Some things we can and do remember, but other things seem to slip through the cracks. By focusing on those things that stick, we can start to place other things into our memory in the same way. In other words, if we can figure out what works, then we can do it on purpose.

Here's a perfect example of how our mind works. When was the last time you read the story "The Three Little Pigs"? I bet it was at least a year (if not many years) ago. You probably have not read a book like this since you were a kid, unless you have young children yourself, in which case you don't read it every night, and at most maybe once or twice in the past year. But even though it was a long time ago I bet you still remember who blew the houses down in the story. You probably also remember the name of the girl who ate the porridge in "The Three Bears" or what kind of animal "Mary" had.

Now let's try some abstract lines. Most people use a computer keyboard at least once a week, if not on a daily basis. Now if you're one of those people, try to answer this question. What symbol is above the number 7 on the keyboard? Is it *, %, or $? Your mind probably looks like a very long curse word, and you probably didn't come up with the right answer. Chances are, even if you did guess right, you're still not sure if it's the right answer. On my keyboard it is the '&' symbol. The point is that some things are easy to remember and some things aren't. Stories are easy to remember.

One way to show how easily things can be remembered with images is to create a story. When we create a story, we are linking information together. Imagine you are at a fair and you are looking for 20 of your friends. If they are spread out all over the grounds, it might take you hours before you find them all. There is also the problem of the 20 friends constantly moving around and not staying in the same place for long. Their constant movement would make it even harder to find them. This experience is like looking for information somewhere in your brain. If you don't put it in a specific place, then you'll be searching for a long time. However, if you knew your best friend was by the Ferris wheel and everyone else was there with her, then you could find all of your friends in just a few minutes. Similarly, you can remember information by putting it in a place where you can find it, a place that exists specifically to hold information.

You are going to try to remember another list of 20 words. Sorry to be bossy, but you did buy this book. To make it easy to find the words in your mind, I am going to tell you where to find your first word, just like I told you where to find your best friend at the fair. I'm also going to clump the rest of the words together, in the same way that all of your friends are standing with your best friend at the Ferris wheel. Learning a list of 20 words in this way is a simple example that will hopefully boost your confidence.

Here is the list of 20 things. Don't memorize it yet. Just read it.

1. knight
2. dragon
3. cave
4. butterflies
5. alien
6. waterfall
7. honey
8. treasure chest
9. bananas
10. sword
11. cactus
12. sheep
13. gum
14. boot
15. balloons
16. rollercoaster
17. pool
18. China
19. thunder
20. spider

To remember this list, we are going to use a story. The story starts with a great knight, the number one knight in all the land. Read the story below to yourself and pay attention to the underlined words. It should you take less than a minute.

> A <u>knight</u> rides a <u>dragon</u> into a <u>cave</u> filled with <u>butterflies</u>. These butterflies start chasing an <u>alien</u> which runs and jumps over a <u>waterfall</u> into a pool of <u>honey</u>. In it the alien finds a <u>treasure chest</u> filled with <u>bananas</u>. Inside one banana the alien finds a <u>sword</u> that he uses to slice open a <u>cactus</u> and lets loose a herd of <u>sheep</u>. The sheep spit out their chewing <u>gum</u> and put on cowboy <u>boots</u>. The sheep then grab some <u>balloons</u> and board a <u>rollercoaster</u> which takes them to a swimming <u>pool</u> in <u>China</u>. Suddenly it <u>thunders</u> and starts to rain <u>spiders</u>.

Now this story seems strange, but that is the point. The more out of the ordinary it is, the more it will stick in the mind. We'll talk more about that later on, but for now try to remember the 20 words by filling in the blanks:

A _____ rides a _____ into a _____ filled with _____. [They] start chasing an _____ which runs and jumps over a _____ into a pool of _____. In it [he] finds a _____ filled with _____. In one [he] finds a _____ that he uses to slice open a _____ and lets loose a herd of _____. (They) are all chewing _____ and wearing cowboy _____. (They) grab some _____ and board a _____ which takes them to a swimming _____ in _____. Suddenly it _____ and starts to rain _____.

Now try to remember the story again on your own. Start with the 'number one', which is the great or number one knight in all the land. This will help you to remember that the number one word is 'knight'. Go ahead. I'll wait here.

If you didn't remember all 20 words, don't worry. You will have lots of practice with making stories. My guess is that you remembered a lot more words than you did on the first list you tried.

A list of information can be in the form of notes for a biology class, an equipment checklist for camping, vocabulary words for a history test, a household chore list, or even a simple shopping list. Some lists will be numbered and some won't. Some will be broken into sets and others will be scattered. Some will be short with simple words and others will be long lists of complex terms. You will be able to remember any list.

Making stories is an important skill to remembering lists and you can use this skill to remember other things.

You can use a image with a shovel to remember a new friend's name is Doug, a story about your dog under a Christmas tree to remember she was born in December, or a story about a disco light on the back of a semi-truck (18-wheeler) to remember a party scheduled for the 18th of the month.

You will only get better at imagining and creating stories to remember information. It seems crazy that something this simple can work, but it does, and it is your first step to world domination.

imagine that.

(I remember Wilson, the volleyball, but I can't remember the other guy's name.)

Whenever I think of Noah, I always think of the Ark.

Our mind remembers things or images more than letters or words. If you think about it, written language was invented to represent things in our world. By nature you are more likely to remember an actual tree than the four letters you use to spell the word. Our mind can more easily imagine a flower than the nine-letter word 'beautiful' that describes it. When you hear the word 'elephant', you are more likely to think of the large, grey-skinned animal from Africa than the string of random letters like 'p', 'e', 'l', 'h', 'a', 't', 'e', and 'n' put together in a specific order because someone chose to give this animal a name.

Because our mind is meant to work with concrete things, it is harder to remember words like 'finance', 'fiction', or 'accept' than it is to remember words like 'alligator', 'hammer', or 'pudding'. The more abstract or intangible a word is, the less likely you are to remember it.

If you have ever seen the movie *Cast Away* with Tom Hanks, then you already understand this. The movie is about a FedEx worker who is stranded on an island with only a volleyball for a friend. At the mention of this, many readers are already saying the volleyball's name, Wilson, which is the brand of volleyball. Now even though most people remember the name 'Wilson', very few people will remember the name of the man stranded on the island. Even though two hours plus is dedicated to this man, few can remember his name. Granted, Wilson's name is said far more often, but remembering the name 'Wilson' for someone shaped like a volleyball is way easier than remembering that the name of the guy who looks like Fabio in the final round of *Celebrity Survivor* is Chuck Noland.

In order to make something easy to remember, it must be turned into an object or image. An object, something you can see and touch, is much easier to remember than a word, or a set of abstract lines. It's just like giving a child a set of blocks to help with the understanding of numbers. When you think of an object, your mind has something to work with and hold on to.

Names are one of the more difficult things to remember. If you try to think of a name as just a string of letters, it will be tough to find it later on. Think of trying to find the word 'top' in a bowl of Alphagetti, a bowl that is big enough to hold all the names you have ever heard. If you change a name into an object, it is much easier to remember it.

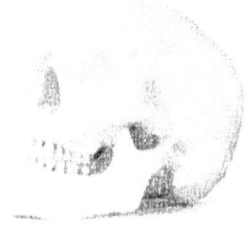

If you used an image of a skull for the name 'Sculley' or a lizard for 'Lizzie', it will make things easier. Finding a skull or lizard in a bowl of Alphagetti is much easier than finding a series of letters. If you are a little OCD, I'm sure you'll find it in seconds. When you change a word or a name into an image, it is a lot easier to put it somewhere in your mind.

There are many ways to turn words (or any piece of information) into a thing or an image. An easy and natural way is to simply use the first image that comes to mind. The first thing I think of when I see the word 'distance' is a measuring tape. Maybe a planet could represent the word 'space'. The word 'memory' could be a brain, a picture frame, or a computer disk. You can use images that work for you.

An image can be a smaller part of a bigger thing or an idea such as a tooth for 'dentistry', a baseball bat for 'sports', or a stethoscope for 'health'. It can be something that sounds similar such as *a glue stick* for 'acoustic' or *ant's chess* for 'anxious'. It could even be something that has the meaning of the word in some way such as a spider for the word 'eight', since it has eight legs; or a cow for the word 'utter'... you know, because it has an udder. There are many different ways to turn words into things.

To remember people you can use images of their name. For Mr. Sarpin, your neighbour who works at the bank, you could imagine a giant serpent (an image for 'Sarpin') coming out of the cash machine at his work and attacking him. For Scott, the quiet kid at the back of class who plays basketball, you could imagine him playing basketball with a roll of toilet paper (since it's 'Scotties' brand). To remember your dentist's last name is Berkowski, you could imagine this dentist working on a shivering cold cow wearing skis (which could be an image for Berkowski (brrr-cow-ski).

For learning vocabulary, using images will make it easier to remember difficult words. Imagining a tiny liver from a cow inside a gold soccer trophy will help you to remember that 'atrophy' is 'a decrease in size of an organ caused by disease or disuse'. Imagining a mosquito (an annoying insect) with a cast around its 'fractured' leg will help you to remember that 'fractious' means 'easily annoyed or irritated'. Imagining an altar boy kneeling near a giant bell at a funeral will help you to remember that 'knell' (sounds like kneel) is 'a sound of a bell rung slowly to announce a death'.

There are many other ways to use images to remember information. Imagining an apple hanging off the middle line of a sheet of music can help you to remember that the note just below the middle line is an 'A' note (since apple starts with 'a'). Imagining a spider using an oxygen mask will help you to remember that oxygen is number '8' on the periodic table of elements (since a spider has 'eight' legs). Imagining Queen Victoria eating a BC apple will help you to remember that Victoria is the capital city of the province of British Columbia (B.C.).

Sound-alikes

Use an image that sounds like the word.

able	table	notion	nation
ask	mask	other	otter
basic	bazooka	prone	prawn
battle	bottle	pull	pole
cost	ghost	role	reel
cover	culvert	scene	sand
due	doe	shallow	swallow
each	peach	size	Zeus
facts	fox	sort	suit
fault	felt	swear	sweater
form	farm	thank	tank
hour	oar	time	dime
issue	a shoe	trial	trail
locate	locket	twice	twist
Midge	match	very	fairy

Characters

Use a character that represents the word.

anger	the Hulk	humble	Wilbur
acceptance	Queen Elsa	inform	Data
adventure	Dr. Jones	insanity	Mad Hatter
amusement	clown	laugh	Fozzie Bear
ancient	King Tut	lead	Captain Picard
arrogance	Babe Ruth	lonely	Wall-E
aware	lifeguard	lost	Orphan Annie
blue	Smurf	magic	Harry Potter
darkness	Batman	nobility	Robin Hood
death	Grim Reaper	passion	Tinkerbell
destiny	Bilbo Baggins	power	Ironman
determine	Terminator	simple	Mater
explain	Bill Nye	space	astronaut
friendship	Woody	truth	Sherlock
honest	Abe Lincoln	wisdom	Yoda

Symbols

Use a symbol for the word.

ancient	pyramid	hope	anchor
ascension	ladder	intelligence	dolphin
beauty	flower	news	bell
birth	egg	night	moon
change	butterfly	passion	fire
connection	chain	patience	turtle
death	skull	peace	olive branch
deception	cloak	pride	lion
decision	crossroad	promise	rainbow
education	apple	rebirth	phoenix
family	wedding ring	reproduce	rabbit
fiction	unicorn	romance	rose
freedom	window	rudeness	donkey
grace	swan	sadness	albatross
hope	anchor	time	clock

Parts

Use a small image for a larger thing or idea.

art	clay	laundry	sock
beach	umbrella	mechanic	wrench
birthday	cake	news	paper
breakfast	cereal	ocean	seahorse
campsite	axe	Olympics	medal
chess	rook	orchestra	violin
China	Great Wall	pond	duck
circus	balloon	restaurant	menu
cowboy	hat	school	desk
curling	rock	science	microscope
desert	cactus	snake	jungle
forest	tree	theatre	popcorn
gym	basketball	traffic	stop sign
Halloween	pumpkin	travel	suitcase
hygiene	toothbrush	zoo	giraffe

directions

Memory Challenge

For this challenge you will practice remembering directions using landmarks and directions like 'east', 'straight', or 'left'. With each challenge, you can use a timer to see how long it takes you to memorize the information. It's a good way to keep track of your success.

Remembering directions is easier if the information is a bright, colourful object. For example, if you need to remember to go east at the statue of a horse and rider, think of 'east' as an Easter egg being kicked by the horse.

When thinking of 'left' you could use autumn 'leaves' to imagine a landmark such as a grain elevator. When you see the elevator while you are driving, you will remember 'leaves' and turn left at this corner. So long as you are not on your phone, daydreaming about your middle school crush, or applying make-up while you're driving, then you should notice the landmarks where you need to turn.

Here are some directions to 'a friend's house':

"Head east past the statue of the general on his horse. After you cross the railroad tracks, turn right. Down this road you'll see a red barn. Head south at this intersection. When you see the windmills you will drive about 10 km until the next turn. At the little church head west until you see the grain elevators where you turn left. Down this gravel road you will cross a bridge. At the next intersection turn north until you come to your first traffic light. Your friend lives in the red house that you see there."

Darren Mark Michalczuk

directions

Cheat Sheet

Imagine:
- The **statue** of a horse and rider kicking an **Easter egg** through some goal posts like a football to remember to turn east at the statue.
- **Writing** poetry on the boxcars of a **train** going by with a giant feather pen to remember to turn right (write) after the railroad crossing.
- A **South** African tree frog climbing the side of a **barn** to remember to head south at the red barn.
- Riders on motorcycles finishing a **10 kilometre race** by jumping over **windmills** to remember you have 10 kilometres to go to reach your friend's house.
- Throwing a **Western** (cowboy) hat onto the steeple of a **church** to remember to head west at the small church.
- Flying over some grain **elevators** on a giant **leaf** like you are hang gliding to remember to turn left at the grain elevators.
- Santa hanging a **stocking** for the troll that lives under the **bridge** to remember to head north after the bridge.
- A **cherry** hanging off of the **traffic light** to remember to look for a red house at the first traffic light.

Darren Mark Michalczuk

You can set a memory alarm.

(Every time something weird happens, I stop and think - which at our house is every few minutes.)

I can memorize 100 digits of pi and the entire periodic table, but I forgot where I put my car keys.

Whenever we get together as a family, inevitably the embarrassing stories from our childhood come out and all the cousins, uncles, and 'special friends' have a good laugh. Over time the details change or get exaggerated, but here is one that I'll try to recount as accurately as I can:

My brother and I grew up on a farm in northern Alberta, Canada. During the summer months we had a lot of free time so we found ways to entertain ourselves. One day we decided to make a boomerang.

Not being native to Australia, we had to look up what a boomerang looked like in a set of encyclopedias in our basement. These dust- and fake-leather-covered books also said you could ask your local farmboy to help you catch a skunk to raise as a pet. Being a local farmboy, I can tell you this isn't true. And it's probably illegal.

After finding the right page, we found some wood and cut out a shape that looked like the black-and-white picture, except it was four times as heavy as it should have been and it didn't have any of the carved edges that an authentic boomerang would have. Essentially we built a giant curved stick. After 20 or 30 throws we realized that it wasn't coming back. Instead of chasing our fancy stick, we decided to play catch since we didn't have anything better to do. It was going ok until my brother, who is six years older and built like a masoned latrine, got an idea. I could tell by the look on his face that it was a great idea.

He thought he wasn't throwing it hard enough. Before he launched our weighted stick in my direction he yelled, "Don't catch this one!" I'm not sure why I only heard the last three words, but I lined up like a kindergarten kid with no glove trying to catch a college pitcher's knuckleball. I didn't have a hope. As the blur of spinning blades came at my head, I held up my elementary school hands to catch it, keeping my 'eye on the ball' like my brother had taught me. At the last second the wind (at least I think it was the wind) lifted the stick just above my hands and it hit me dead centre on my forehead. I don't know if my feet lifted off the ground like in the story my family tells, but I do know it was the first and only time I was knocked unconscious. I also heard it was the first and only time my brother ran away from home. He left me there on the grass and just ran into the field. He eventually came back and now we have a good story to laugh about.

When I get together with friends I love sharing stories like this, but sometimes they slip my mind. I'll think of a great story about peeing on an electric fence, snorting chocolate milk out my nose in front of my crush, or losing my trunks in the pool. I'll wait for a break in the conversation, which often takes a while with my friends. While someone is blah-blah-blahing about their kid, job, or cat

I start thinking about something else and soon I've forgotten what I was going to say. I'll have a great story about my son going head-first into a swamp with his dirt bike, but by the time I'm done listening to Lisa tell me about how her cat tries to open the cupboard door with her 'cute little paws', all I'm thinking about is groceries. To hold onto thoughts, whether they are practical or just for entertainment, I started using things around me as a 'memory palace'. I place the information where I can find it.

Thoughts

When I want to remember the story about the boomerang I might imagine throwing a boomerang at the TV in the room. The next time I look around the room and see the TV, I'll remember the painful childhood trauma that bonded my brother and me. I might also imagine a tiny dirt biker riding around the coffee table to remember the story about my son not paying attention and driving head-first into a swamp and how he didn't let go of his bike until he was completely underwater. I might also imagine a giant eyeball hanging from the light on the ceiling to remember to compliment someone on their new contact lenses. When there is a break in the conversation I still remember these thoughts and can finally share *my* super-important stuff.

Pocket Alarms

I often carry a few small items in my pocket and use these to trigger my memory to do a few things throughout the day. While sitting down I remember I have to take medicine for my ear infection. Getting up off the couch is hard though, and I'm usually in the middle of an episode of *Game of Thrones* by the time I remember. I imagine using my keys, which are in my pocket, to unlock an Egyptian puzzle box full of pills. After I get up off the couch, the next time I reach in my pocket and feel my keys I will remember to take my pills. You'd think the constant pain in my ear would be enough to remind me, but I have a lot to think about.

I pick up my wallet and remember the story about it being full of cat food to remember to feed my cats, Grizz and Cy. I feel a small tube of lip balm and remember I used it to draw a picture of a baby penguin doing the Macarena on the trash bag. I remember this was a story to remind me to take out the trash.

Alarm Alarm

(No, this isn't a typo. Just an attempt at being clever.) Mornings at our house are quite rushed (as we all like our sleep) but we do our best to remember everything we need for the day. Sometimes there are things that are outside of our routine so I'll set a memory alarm on my alarm clock. On my nightstand I will put something that doesn't belong. For example, I might put a sock on my alarm clock at night. In the morning when I see the out-of-place sock, I will remember the story about finding this sock in a cupcake and then remember I need to take the cupcakes out of the fridge to take to school for my daughter's Halloween party.

I might turn a picture sideways and imagine it pouring soup (that I need to put in the slow cooker) onto the floor. I may put a shampoo bottle from the bathroom in the middle of the bathroom floor and imagine bubbles floating out of it into the dryer (that I need to turn on in the morning). When I wake up and see an item out of place, I stop and think and wonder what clown was messing around in my house. For a brief moment I think maybe my grandmother got into the peach schnapps late the night before and moved things around while telling a story about the good-old-days. Maybe one of my children was sleep-walking and acted out dreams of playing hide-and-seek with laundry. Or it could have been a crafty raccoon with a mischievous side. I quickly realize, however, that I made a story to remember something important, as much as cupcakes can be important.

I got in the habit of finding an object to store information where I needed one. A clock that I would eventually look at, a book that I routinely pick up, or a coat that I would have to put on would all become places where I would put a picture of something I needed to remember.

i've experienced the 'butterfly effect'.

(Memory skills helped me make one small decision, and my life changed forever because of it.)

I wasn't sure if I could save someone's life, but I did know the alphabet really well.

When I was younger, I was a lifeguard. I started working at our local swimming pool in Athabasca when I was in high school. While attending college and university I worked at some of the pools that were run by the City of Edmonton such as Londonderry and Mill Creek. During the summer I worked at other pools such as Miette Hot Springs, beautiful naturally heated pools in the Rockies; West Edmonton Mall Waterpark, the largest indoor water park in the world at the time; and Fort Good Hope, a small pool I literally had to build inside a small warehouse for a small town of about 600 near the Arctic Circle. In total I worked at 13 different pools and had the time of my life.

I share this with you because I was able to do this amazing job in part due to my memory skills. Of course I had to learn to swim, have fun with kids, and understand basic water chemistry, but a big part of my job was First Aid.

Being responsible for the people in a pool means you have to know how to treat injuries or respond to emergencies, and if possible prevent them. For most of what I had to learn I used memory skills to remember the important information so that I could focus on other things, like should I wear boxers or briefs?

Now I will share with you some details about my training. Please be aware that this will in no way train or prepare you for doing First Aid. This sounds like common sense, but you'd be surprised how many people think they can do medical operations after watching reruns of *ER*. I actually had a teacher who watched an episode of *M*A*S*H* (a TV show about a medical unit during war times) and used the information from the show to teach us how to do a tracheotomy. I wish I was making this up, but it's etched in my memory. He was an awesome teacher, but he just got a little too excited about teaching us medical practices from a Thursday night show. Please take a course from trained professionals to learn First Aid. It's well worth it.

When you come across an accident or emergency there are certain things you must check for. Of course you cannot put yourself or the injured person in danger or cause more damage. If this person is unconscious, then my job as a responder is to check for any life-threatening injuries, get help, and treat what I can. Some things are more serious and should be checked and treated before others. For example, a cut on a leg is not as serious as a blocked airway. A person who does not take in oxygen will have brain or cell damage within minutes, and so this emergency must be treated before a cut.

In most First Aid classes they teach the ABC's. 'A' stands for Airway, which is the first thing you must check as a first responder. If the airway is not open, then the person cannot breathe - and this is a serious problem. If the airway is open, then the next thing to check is the breathing. A person might stop breathing for a variety of reasons such as electrocution, allergic reaction, or heart attack. 'B' is for breathing, which is the next thing to check. After this, 'C' stands for circulation, or checking someone's pulse to make sure that their heart is beating. Things that affect these ABC's are life-threatening and must be checked and treated first. Emergency Services such as an ambulance or hospital also need to be contacted.

Using this idea of each letter (ABC) standing for something to look for as a lifeguard made sense, so I tried applying this technique with the rest of the 'checklist' by using ABCDEFGHI. This took me some time to figure out and it just happened to work out. It isn't something I would do now since I have other strategies, but as a kid this seemed to be a genius way of remembering.

Here is my 'First Aid Alphabet':

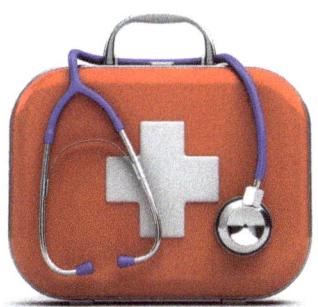

Life-Threatening

- A   Airway
- B   Breathing
- C   Circulation

Could be Life-Threatening

- D   Deadly Bleeding (big cuts that could get worse)
- E   Emergency Medic Alerts (for diabetes or life-threatening allergies that require a medical bracelet)

- F   Fractures (for 'breaks' to the femur, back, or neck - I put 'breaks' in quotation marks because I can't tell if something is broken; only a doctor can)

Might be Life-Threatening

- G   Get Vitals (anything wrong with the vital signs - including eyes, breath, or pulse - would show something is wrong with the person)
- H   Head to Toe Survey (check everything from head to toe by hand - well, almost everything; we were lifeguards, not doctors)
- I   Incident Report (documenting the incident for paramedics, pool records, or just plain busy work)

This alphabet helped me to pass a lot of my life saving courses and gave me the confidence to help during emergencies. Within my first year of working in pools I started competing in 'lifeguard competitions'. I used this alphabet as a way to get through each test situation. Of the four or five events in each competition, all but one was scored on how well you recognize, check, and treat the injuries on this list. When I was 16, after training for a few weeks we competed in Hinton, Alberta and got second place, losing only to a senior team that had to drop from the 'A' event because some members had been disqualified. For the next few years I coached lifeguarding teams, at times having by far the largest 'lifeguard club' in the city. In my final year I decided to compete in the 'A' event with a good friend, Sheldon Shukaliuk. We practiced for a total of 30 minutes, most of which consisted of chatting about cars overtop of a co-worker strapped to a spine board. Although we had very little official practice, we had a strong foundation built around this 'memory' alphabet. Our team name was the 'Security Guards' and we won first place at provincials. Go Team!

Though it was cool to win, it was cooler to work at so many pools with so many amazing people. I could have easily worked at a chicken farm across the field from my parents' farm in Rochester, which would have been a good, honest job, but I decided to become a lifeguard instead. I still remember the day I had to decide between working a mile from home doing simple labour or driving to town to be responsible for a pool full of ADD kids.

The memory skills allowed me to take a risk on a job that has allowed me to see the Northern Lights in the Arctic Circle where I was hired to build a pool for a small Native community. I was able to watch bighorn sheep graze on Pyramid Mountain near Jasper while I guarded at Miette Hot Springs. I was also part of a human chain sliding down 'Twister' at West Edmonton Mall's World Waterpark earning $6.20 an hour as a wave pool guard.

The 'Butterfly Effect' is the idea that a very small event can have a very large, complex effect. For example, the flap of a butterfly's wings could lead to a change of events that could cause a windstorm on the other side of the ocean. Had I not been able to get through my lifeguarding courses so easily, maybe instead of working poolside with wonderful people I would have worked for a chicken farmer and faced insults and abuse from PETA protesters for years to come. Either way, I am thankful for my memory skills.

Your Mind is a Palace.

(I can always remember where I put my keys if I put them on the hook at the top of the stairs.)

If you want to find the pitcher at a baseball game, look on the clay mound in the middle of a baseball diamond.

Now that we are familiar with using objects or images to remember information, I would like to teach you how to use a memory palace. This is a very cool way of remembering information with a long history. I will try to show you where this comes from, who has used it, and how to advance this concept to make it easier to use.

First of all, there is a legend (or maybe a true story) that a Greek poet, Simonides of Ceos, invented the technique after attending a banquet that went horribly wrong. Simonides, as the entertainment for the event, was up on stage performing with a great view of the floor and all of the guests. As the story goes, he had stepped outside to meet some friends. Soon after this, the hall he was performing in suddenly collapsed, killing everyone inside. The bodies were so damaged from the fallen building that those killed could not even be recognized by loved ones.

Simonides was able to help people find their fallen family members by remembering where they were at the moment just before he left the hall. Because he had been watching the guests just before he stepped outside, he knew where everyone was under the rubble.

For example, maybe Simonides remembered Alexander standing by the table of food. By searching through the rubble to find the table, Alexander's family was able to find his body. Maybe Simonides remembered seeing Katherine by the vase of flowers on the east wall. Finding the broken vase with flowers under the rubble would help her family find her body. Maybe Simonides remembered Sophia near the stairs waiting for a friend. Sophia's father then would know to look at the top of the stairs to find his daughter's body. Essentially, Simonides was able to identify all (or at least most) of the bodies by using specific objects that had specific locations around the room.

Whether or not this is the true origin of the memory palace technique, it is a really good way to explain it. In this example Simonides was familiar with the hall and was able to place information, in this case people, into places he was familiar with. This is how the 'Memory Palace' technique works.

At some point people started creating their own memory palaces and placing other information besides people into these places. I will use a prince who wants to remember the next day's to-do list as an example of a memory palace. This prince uses a special room that he calls the crown room as a place to remember things. This room has objects in specific locations that are familiar to him.

First, at the entrance, there is a door carved from mahogany wood. In front of this door there is a rug with a beautiful design of mountains woven into it. Next to this rug is an oak chair. To the right of this chair is a tall, leafy plant that is beginning to bloom. Above the plant there is a beautifully framed mirror hanging on the wall. There are more objects around the crown room that he can always remember in a very specific order. In the prince's mind the objects never change, and neither do their location.

The prince has several things that he needs to remember to do the next day. The first thing he needs to remember is to feed his horse. To remember this he places this information in the first place in his crown room. He imagines horses crashing in through the front door. Since the objects in the room are always the same, the prince knows exactly where he needs to look to remember what he needs to do the next day. When he looks at his first location, which is the door, he remembers from the story he has created that he has to feed his horse.

He does the same for the second task he has to remember, which is to sharpen his sword. He imagines using his sword to chop up the elaborate rug in front of the door. When he thinks of his second object in his 'memory palace', which is the rug, he thinks of the story that involves his sword and then he remembers that he must get his sword sharpened.

He continues to make stories with the objects in his memory palace. On the chair (the third object) he imagines a queen's crown spinning so that he can remember to meet with his mother. He imagines blood dripping down from the leaves of the plant as a reminder to talk to one of his soldiers who was badly injured in battle. In the mirror he imagines seeing a woman wearing a dress made of letters as a reminder to send an important letter to the princess from the neighbouring kingdom.

You can create a memory palace from a place that is familiar. It can be a path that you walk regularly with the objects along the way acting as 'memory hooks'. It can be a path through work or school. It can be a routine drive, or it can be objects in a relative's yard. A memory palace is basically a path or a place with objects that you are familiar with.

People are often encouraged to use objects from rooms in a house. One hundred is a common number, made from ten rooms with ten objects in each room. This will give you one hundred places to store information. It will also give you an image for all two-digit numbers from 00 to 99 (or from 1 to 100).

Though this is a good system to use, there are some limitations. One problem is that not everyone has ten rooms with ten unique objects in each room. If I tried using one of my rooms in college, it would have a light switch, a jar of mustard, a CD case, and not much else. Other people might have too many objects to choose from, possibly because of being a collector or maybe a hoarder.

Objects may also start to blur together in the mind because of being too similar. A stereo, TV, computer, and microwave are all rectangular, electronic appliances. When memorizing, the more unique the objects are, the easier it will be to keep them separate in your memory.

Another drawback is that the layout of rooms in your own house may change over time. You might replace a chair, move a painting, or throw away your coffee table's centrepiece. Not everyone has a room they can keep specifically as a 'think' room.

You can imagine a room being 'frozen in time' to keep all the objects the same, such as a room from your childhood. You can also design the room in your mind any way you want. When I teach memory skills I use the same palaces to start with. Should someone want to create their own later on, they will simply have more places to store information.

The memory palaces I use aren't exactly rooms but a collection of objects from one place or theme. Each one is like a hybrid of a palace and peg list (a list of numbered objects). The objects are in a specific order because each one has a number connected with it. The first 'memory palace' has ten objects that children are familiar with. Each has a connection based on visual, auditory, or kinesthetic cues. Each one also has a colour connection, giving you one more connection to make it easier to find in your mind.

Kids Palace

I have many different 'memory palaces', but each one is similar and easy to understand. Instead of using rooms in a house, I use different locations such as a school, a car, and a beach. Each one has exactly ten items, each of which is numbered in the mind. In the prince's memory palace, he would have to count around the room to find the number of each object. For example, he would have to count the door, the rug, the chair, and the plant before he knew the mirror was the number '5' object, like finger counting.

In the Kids Palace, a palace filled with things that are familiar to kids, each object has a number attached to it. For example, the '3' object is a tricycle because it has 3 wheels (a kinaesthetic cue), handlebars that are shaped like a 3 (a visual cue), and it's called a 3-wheeler (an auditory cue). It also has a main colour connected with it: red. These are the same cues that will help you to remember the other objects in this 'memory room' and other rooms. I will explain the objects in this room thoroughly below. Why not? I've got time. This palace should be practiced until you know it well. The picture for each number should come into your mind instantly. You can practice through the day while you are on hold, at a red light, or listening to a story about someone's cat. The better you know this list, the better it will work in your mind.

1 BANANA
The '1' object is a banana because it has '1' peel, it is shaped like a 1, and it is 'sun' yellow ('sun' rhymes with '1'). Its colour is yellow.

2 DOLPHIN
The '2' object is a dolphin because it has '2' fins, it has a fin shaped like a '2', and it is 'blue' (rhymes with '2'). Its colour is blue.

3 TRICYCLE

The '3' object is a tricycle since it has '3' wheels, handlebars shaped like a '3', and it is called a '3'-wheeler. Its colour is red.

4 KITE

The '4' object is a kite because it has '4' sides, it is shaped like a '4', and it is a '4'-sided kite. Its colour is purple/pink.

5 BOXING GLOVE

The '5' object is a boxing glove since it has 5 fingers, it is shaped like a '5', and it is part of a 'live' sport (since 'live' rhymes with 'five'). Its colour is orange or gold.

6 BASEBALL CAP

The '6' object is a baseball cap because it has '6' sections, it is shaped like a '6', and it is a 'Sixers' cap. Its colour is green.

7 BOOK

The '7' object is a book since it is about '7' dwarfs, it is shaped like a '7', and it is called *'The 7 Dwarfs'*. Its colour is brown.

8 SPIDER

The '8' object is a spider because it has '8' legs, its body is shaped like an '8', and kids 'hate' (which rhymes with 8) it. Its colour is black.

9 GOLF CLUB

The '9' object is a golf club because there are '9' in a set, it's shaped like a '9', and it's called a '9' iron. Its colour is grey.

10 BOWLING SET

The '10' object is a bowling set because it has '10' pins, it is shaped like a '10'(pin / ball), and it is '10' pin bowling. Its colour is white.

brain magic 51

Movies

Memory Challenge

Here is a list of the top ten movies for gross box office sales (as of 2016). This list will definitely change, mainly because Hollywood hasn't made a full length movie featuring funny cat fails or the Teletubbies. For now, here is the list you will memorize:

1. *Avatar*
2. *Titanic*
3. *Jurassic World*
4. *The Avengers*
5. *Furious 7*
6. *Avengers: Age of Ultron*
7. *Harry Potter and the Deathly Hallows - Part 2*
8. *Frozen*
9. *Iron Man 3*
10. *Transformers: Dark of the Moon*

Now that you know the Kids Palace well, you can use stories to remember lists like grocery items, course notes, or chapters in a book. I had to repeat this point because it is a really important concept. Plus I had some extra space on this page.

Some lists can be for practice while others can be put toward practical use. Don't worry; you can reuse the Kid's Palace over and over. As you practice more and get better at remembering images, you'll be able to find the information you are looking for. Trust me. Or don't. You can decide for yourself.

See if you can remember the top ten movies by making a simple story with the each of the 10 objects from the Kids Palace list. Good luck.

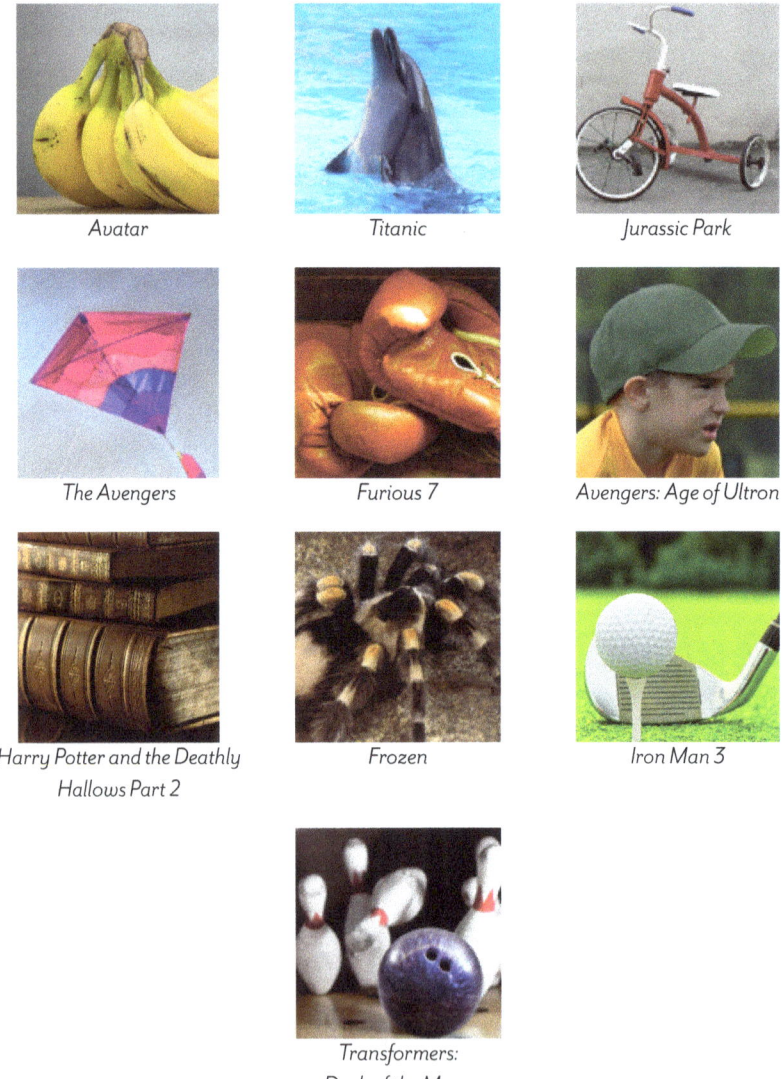

Avatar

Titanic

Jurassic Park

The Avengers

Furious 7

Avengers: Age of Ultron

Harry Potter and the Deathly Hallows Part 2

Frozen

Iron Man 3

Transformers: Dark of the Moon

Darren Mark Michalczuk

#1 *Avatar*: To remember the #1 movie on the list, imagine a blue 'Avatar' from the movie diving into a pile of bananas. Then, whenever you look in the #1 place in the Kid's Palace, which is the banana, you'll remember the story and that *Avatar* is the top grossing movie of all time.

#2 *Titanic*: Imagine a **dolphin** (2) diving down into the ocean and searching through the sunken **'Titanic'**.

#3 *Jurassic World*: Imagine riding a **tricycle** (3) through the tourist area of **'Jurassic World'**. See dinosaurs emerging from behind trees, hear them roar, and imagine you are pedaling faster. The more details you include, the more you'll remember.

#4 *The Avengers*: Imagine flying a **kite** (4) that is being attacked **by the Avengers** like the Hulk and Captain America.

#5 *Furious 7*: Imagine using **boxing gloves** (5) to fight **seven furious** bulls in a rodeo arena.

#6 *Age of Ultron*: Imagine Avengers riding dinosaurs (**age**) decorated with electronic tubes (**tron**) wearing caps (6).

#7 *The Avengers*: Imagine **Harry Potter** making a **book** (7) fly in the air using a leviosa spell.

#8 *Frozen*: Imagine finding a **frozen** giant **spider** (8) in the freezer next to the turkey and ice pops.

#9 *Iron Man 3*: Imagine **Iron Man** playing his final round of golf with a nine iron **golf club** (9) from the rough.

#10 *Transformers*: Imagine **Transformers** throwing **bowling balls** (10) into space from the dark side of the moon.

 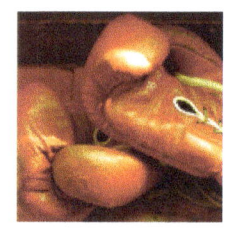 

brain magic

the teens

When you add the Teens on to the Kids Palace, you will have a list with 20 items which gives you more places to store information. Once you have memorized these objects, you will have a set of 20 memory places to remember things. Make sure you take time to learn these well before you use them to remember other things. These objects will become part of your mind and something you will be able to use over and over again for years. This set of objects will be like an organized storage shelf in your mind.

In the Teen Palace, each object has the same connection that the Kids Palace has. For example, the '13' object is the deck of cards because there are 13 cards in each suit, just like the tricycle has 3 wheels. It is also red, just like the tricycle. All of the objects are connected to the number and have a dominant colour, just like the objects in the Kids Palace.

11 FOOTBALL HELMET

There are 11 players on a football team and the face mask has two bars that look like an '11'. *(It's yellow like the banana which also ends with 1.)*

12 EGGS

There are 12 eggs in a carton. *(It's blue like the dolphin.)*

13 CARDS

There are 13 cards in each suit in a deck of cards (from A to K). *(They are also red like the tricycle.)*

14 DIAMOND RING

A diamond has 14 carats and is usually given out on February 14th. *(It is also purple like the kite).*

15 BADMINTON BIRDIE

There are 15 points in a badminton game. *(It's also orange like the boxing gloves.)*

16 FROG

There are 16 toes on a frog (four feet with four toes on each foot). *(It's also green like the baseball cap.)*

17 FOOTBALL

There are 17 holes on a football (16 from the 8 stitches and 1 from the valve). *(It's also brown like the book.)*

18 SEMI

There are 18 wheels on a semi. *(It's also black like a spider.)*

19 GOLF CART

There are 19 holes on a golf course (including the clubhouse). *(It's also grey like the golf club.)*

20 DART

There are 20 numbers on a dartboard. *(It also has white feathers like the bowling pins.)*

Another way of looking at these objects is to call them a 'peg' list. Other peg lists connect the numbers to each object in different ways. If you wanted to create your own memory palace using a peg list, you would only need to have one connection that works for you. You could have objects that rhyme (1-sun, 2-shoe, 3-tree, 4-door, 5-hive …); objects that are shaped like the number (1-bat, 2-swan, 3-heart, 4-sail, 5-hook …); or objects that have things you can count (1-leaf, 2-jeans, 3-ant, 4-wagon, 5-glove …). This gets tricky after 10 and really tricky after 20, but a memory palace with 20 places will hold a lot of information.

Household Items

Memory Challenge

For this challenge you are going to memorize a list of household items.

Your family has listed the items you need to get *out-of-order* and you must memorize all 20 items 'in the right order'. You would never need to remember a scrambled grocery list unless you have quintuplets of kindergarten age who haven't learned to count yet, but it's still good practice. By using the *Kids Palace* (with the Teens) you can imagine each item from the list with the object for each number.

On the next page, each item that you need to remember has the 'memory object' placed above it so that you know where to store it in your mind with a story. When you try to recall these 20 things, you will go to the memory objects in the right order, starting with number one: banana.

Before you start, make sure you know all 20 memory hooks well. This will make it easier to use them for memorizing the list below. You should be able to go through the list from banana to dart in less than 30 seconds.

Remember, your stories should be bright and colourful, out of the ordinary, and funny. Try to see the stories come to life as clearly as you can. It will get easier with practice.

18. apples	13. butter	10. light bulbs	7. DVD
9. keys	15. flowers	6. salmon	4. battery
5. cookies	20. cups	11. ketchup	3. soap
16. Band-Aid	2. socks	17. newspaper	12. coins
1. nails	8. envelopes	14. gum	19. cereal

#18 apples	#13 butter	#10 light bulbs	#7 DVD
#9 keys	#15 flowers	#6 salmon	#4 battery
#5 cookies	#20 cups	#11 ketchup	#3 soap
#16 Band-Aid	#2 socks	#17 newspaper	#12 coins
#1 nails	#8 envelopes	#14 gum	#19 cereal

Darren Mark Michalczuk

Household Items

Cheat Sheet

18 *(app·les)*   Drive a semi-truck (18) through a pile of **apples**.
13 *(but·ter)*   Throw cards (13) ninja-style into a block of **butter**.
10 *(light·bulbs)* Break **light bulbs** in the kitchen with a bowling ball (10).
7 *(mov·ie)*   Watch a **movie** play above a book (7) like a hologram.
9 *(keys)*   Drive silver **keys** in the pond with your nine iron (9).
15 *(flow·ers)*   Place a bouquet of **flowers** in a badminton bird (15).
6 *(sal·mon)*   Scoop a **salmon** from the river with your ball cap (6).
4 *(bat·ter·ies)*   Make a **kite** (4) light up by connecting it to a battery.
5 *(dough)*   Mix **cookie dough** with your boxing gloves (5).
20 *(cups)*   Poke holes in your best **cup** with a dart (20).
11 *(ket·chup)*   Hit a giant bottle of **ketchup** wearing your helmet (18).
3 *(soap)*   Clean the tricycle (3) with bubbly **soap**.
16 *(Band·Aids)*   Help a wounded frog (16) with **Band-Aids**.
2 *(socks)*   Ride a dolphin (2) that jumps for a **sock** above a pool.
17 *(pap·er)*   Kick a football (17) through a **newspaper**.
12 *(coins)*   Crack eggs (12) to find valuable **coins** hidden inside.
1 *(nails)*   Pound **nails** to hold a banana (1) onto a wall.
8 *(en·vel·opes)*   Put a spider (8) in an **envelope** and mail it home.
14 *(gum)*   Stick a diamond ring (14) under a chair with a wad of chewing **gum**.
19 *(cer·e·al)*   Watch an eagle (19) pick **cereal** loops from the sea.

the rest of 'my mind'

(With numbered rooms, lots of space, and colour-coded shelves, anyone's mind can be organized.)

If I'm going to remember more stuff, I'm going to need more rooms… and shelves.

Putting information into the mind is like putting stuff onto shelves or hooks. The more places you have to put information, the more information you will be able to hold. With the 'Kids Palace' (including the Teen Palace) you have 20 shelves or memory hooks that can hold information. You will need to learn the objects in these palaces well. The better you know the images, the easier it will be to use them.

One way to create more memory places is to use a house. By choosing 10 rooms in a house, each with 10 objects to use as hooks, you can create 100 places to put information. As mentioned before, maybe you don't have 10 unique rooms or 10 unique objects in each room. Maybe you are a lone wolf who has only a kitchen, a bathroom, and a bedroom. Maybe the only permanent objects in your tiny cabin in the Alaskan wilderness are a survival knife, a half-empty jar of mustard, and an Operation game with three pieces missing. I don't know your living situation and I don't want to know. Please don't tell me about it.

But you can create places in your mind that have organized objects in your mind, no matter your living situation. Everyone has been in a car. You probably own a car, have a friend who has one, or have seen one in a magazine or on TV. You can create a memory palace by using a car. What's even cooler is that you can choose any car in the world. The make, model, year, and custom features are completely within your control. After all, it is *your* imagination.

To create 100 places to store information, you are going to imagine 10 palaces. It is kin like having rooms, but 'palaces' is a better word to describe them. Once you have these palaces marked in your mind, then you will fill them with unique objects that are easy to find. They are places you either are familiar with or can become familiar with easily. These palaces are a store, a campsite, a car, a school, a farm, a house, a gym, and a beach. Each of these palaces has a list of 10 things that have number connections, just like the Kids Palace. For example, every third object is red and is either shaped like a '3' or has '3' things you can count.

How you imagine these in your mind is up to you. For example, the car can be a 1968 Ford Mustang, a 1957 Chevy, or even a 1938 Dodge truck. It can be in a garage, on the driveway, or in a showroom. It can be a brand new model or an older one gifted to you by a family member (like that cool uncle who lives on someone else's couch). The images I have created are the ones that work for me. To make this image work for memory it has to have four wheels (obviously) and be purple, since this is the colour for all number 4's.

The objects from the "Car Palace" can either be part of one room such as a garage or still be connected to the car. The car seat can either be still in the vehicle or it may be on the floor of the garage. The windshield can be leaning against the garage wall or still be on the car. The screwdriver can be in the toolbox in the trunk, on the shelf of the garage, or simply a floating object in your mind.

These objects will all be held or connected together because you know they are all part of the car. Even though you may have an old, red screwdriver in the junk drawer of your house bent to look like a '7', you imagine a yellow one that is straight like a '1' as part of your 'car' memory palace.

Mega Palace

From these sets of 10, you can build a list of 100 memory objects in your mind. This is a list you can use to remember up to 100 things, or you can use the images to remember things like phone numbers or dates. We'll get to that soon, but for now, here is what the list of 100 things will look like when you are done learning the palaces.

*Just a note, if you ever need an image for 00, you can use the skeleton or a baseball since it looks like a '0'.

00 baseball			
01 banana	26 pop cans	51 pencil	76 hose
02 dolphin	27 phone	52 globe	77 clock
03 tricycle	28 umbrella	53 flag	78 outlet
04 kite	29 battery	54 locker	79 cat
05 glove	30 tent	55 basketball	80 scoreclock
06 ball cap	31 flashlight	56 sharpener	81 bat
07 book	32 backpack	57 piano	82 dumbbell
08 spider	33 ant	58 chess set	83 net
09 golf club	34 butterfly	59 scissors	84 board
10 bowling set	35 flower	60 tractor	85 glove
11 helmet	36 bag	61 bale	86 pool table
12 eggs	37 axe	62 blue jay	87 stick
13 cards	38 binoculars	63 barrel	88 blades
14 ring	39 frying pan	64 pig	89 whistle
15 birdie	40 car	65 pitchfork	90 shell
16 frog	41 tool	66 cricket	91 paddle
17 football	42 windshield	67 boot	92 flippers
18 semi	43 traffic lights	68 bull	93 lifejacket
19 golf cart	44 engine	69 windmill	94 sailboat
20 basket	45 tire	70 house	95 starfish
21 hydrant	46 radio	71 broom	96 turtle
22 bench	47 seat	72 window	97 boomer
23 slush cup	48 wheel	73 couch	98 sunglasses
24 stroller	49 key	74 bed	99 rod
25 coffee pot	50 bus	75 fan	100 skeleton

These are the palaces you'll learn.

store palace

The second memory palace is the store. This will extend your list up to 29 places to store information in your mind. This palace contains the numbers from 20 to 29.

SHOPPING BASKET

The 'marker' object for the corner store (a convenience store like 7-Eleven) is the shopping basket. The basket is blue and has '2' handles. This will help you to remember that the store is the second 'memory place' and any object in it starts with '2'.

21 FIRE HYDRANT

The fire hydrant in the camp is shaped like a '1' (and it's yellow like the banana). This means that the hydrant is the 21st memory hook. It is '2_' because it is from the corner store and '1' because it is shaped like a '1').

22 BENCH

A bench has '2' legs (and is blue like the dolphin).

23 SLUSH CUP

The slush cup comes in '3' sizes (and is red like the tricycle).

24 STROLLER

A baby stroller has '4' wheels (and is purple like the kite).

25 COFFEE POT

The coffee pot is shaped like a '5' (and is orange like the boxing gloves).

26 TOY ARMY MEN

Army men use '6-shooters' (and are green like the baseball cap).

27 PHONE

The phone uses sets of '7' numbers (and is brown like the book).

28 UMBRELLA

The umbrella has '8' sections (and is black like the spider).

29 BATTERY

The battery has '9' volts (and is grey like the golf club).

SAFE

The safe has a handle and is dial-shaped like a '10'. It is white like the bowling pins. The 10th object on each list isn't used when counting from 0 to 100, but I include it anyway.

If you want to use the "Store" memory place as a stand-alone list, here are the objects and the number connections:

1.	hydrant	6.	pop cans
2.	bench	7.	phone
3.	slush cup	8.	umbrella
4.	stroller	9.	battery
5.	coffee pot	10.	*safe*

A memory palace can also be any building you are familiar with. The objects in or around the building can be places to store information. A church, a barn, a garage, a shed, or a trailer could all be used as memory palaces. The objects don't have to have a number connection. The location of each object could be a way to remember them. A rug in a church could the first object because it is the first thing you see. A saddle in a barn could be the sixth thing you see as you walk around.

brain magic

73

Camp Palace

The third memory palace is the campsite. This is the next set of 'memory objects' that will extend your list up to roughly 40 places. This palace contains the numbers from 30 to 39. These are all things that you might use or see when enjoying the great outdoors.

This palace contains the numbers from 30 to 39.

30 TENT
The marker for the camp is the tent. The tent is red and has '3' poles. This will help you to remember that the camp is the third 'memory place' and any objects in it start with '3'.

31 FLASHLIGHT
The flashlight in the camp is shaped like a '1' (and it's yellow like the banana). This means that the flashlight is the 31st memory hook. It is '3_' because it is from the camp and '1' because it is shaped like a '1'.

32 BACKPACK
A backpack has '2' straps (and is blue like the dolphin).

33 ANT
The ant has '3' body sections (and is red like the tricycle).

34 BUTTERFLY
A butterfly has '4' wing sections (and is purple like the kite).

35 FLOWER
The flower has '5' sections (and is orange like the boxing gloves).

36 SLEEPING BAG
The sleeping bag is wrapped up like a '6' (and is green like the baseball cap).

37 **AXE**

The axe is shaped like a '7' (and is brown like the book).

38 **BINOCULARS**

The binoculars look like an '8' at the end (and they are black like the spider) so they are '38'.

39 **FRYING PAN**

The frying pan is shaped like a '9' (and is grey like the golf club) so it's '39'.

The compass has a dial and handle that are together shaped like a '10' (and it is white like the bowling pins). (Remember that the 10th object on each list isn't used when counting from 0 to 100, but I include it here anyway.)

If you haven't skipped to another chapter because this is too hard, you should do so now. Seriously.

If you use 'The Camp' memory place as a stand-alone list, here are the object and number connections:

1.	flashlight	6.	sleeping bag
2.	backpack	7.	axe
3.	ant	8.	binoculars
4.	butterfly	9.	frying pan
5.	flower	10.	*compass*

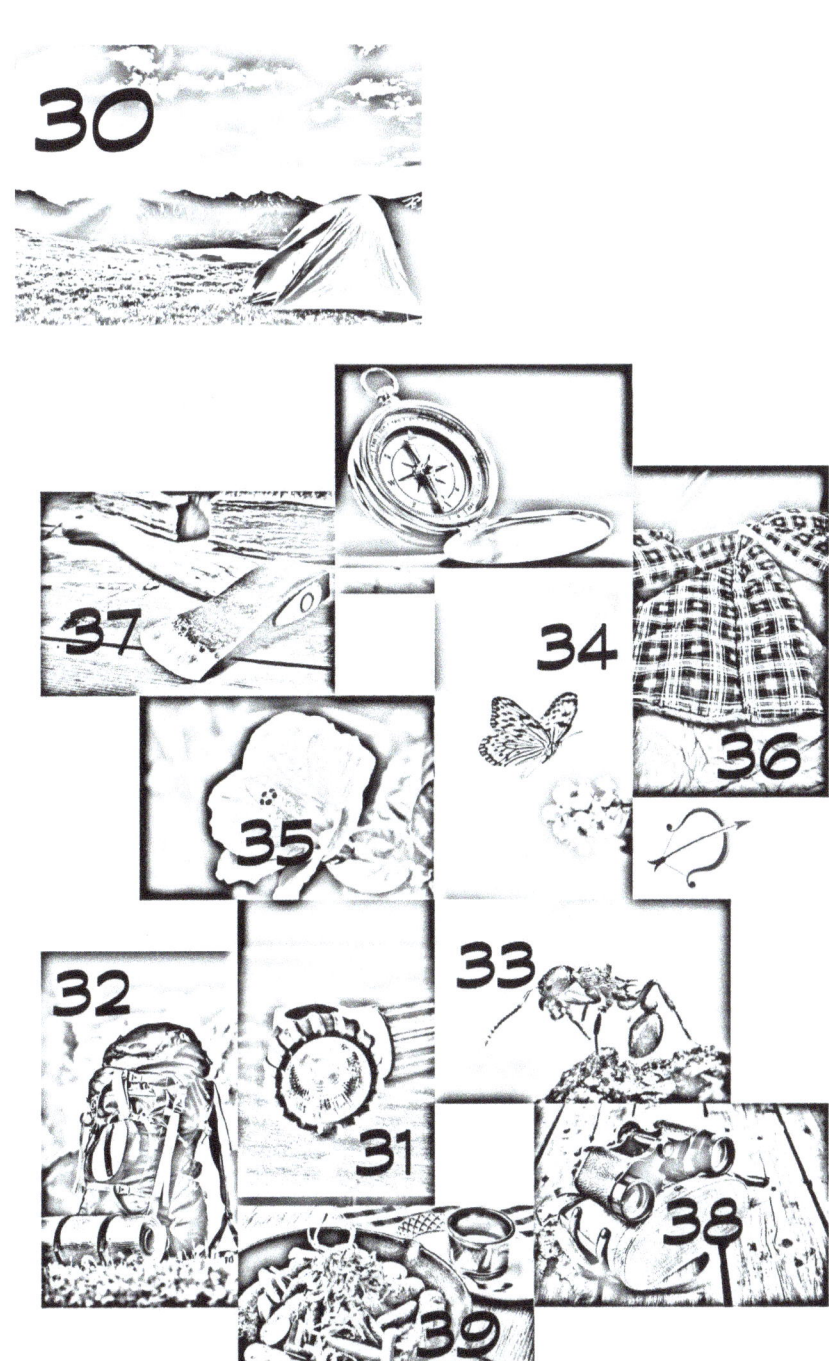

car palace

The fourth memory palace is the corner store. This is the next set of 'memory objects' that will extend your list up to roughly 50 places. This palace contains the numbers from 40 to 49. With this you can memorize the list of presidents of the United States. I am writing this section two days after President Trump's inauguration, so I'm going to have to come up with a cool story about his hair and a car tire.

This palace contains the numbers from 40 to 49.

40 CAR

The car is purple and has '4' poles, so it's '40'. This will help you to remember that the car is the fourth 'memory place' and any object in it starts with '4'.

41 SCREWDRIVER

The screwdriver is shaped like a '1' (and it's yellow like the banana). This means that the screwdriver is the 41st memory hook. It is '4_' because it is from the camp and '1' because it is shaped like a '1'.

42 WINDSHIELD

A windshield from camp has '2' wipers (and looks blue from the sky like the dolphin).

43 TRAFFIC LIGHTS

There are '3' colours on a traffic light; red, green and yellow (and the light is often red like the tricycle).

44 ENGINE

The engine has '4' cylinders (and it is purple like the kite).

45 TIRE

The tire has '5' sections (and it is gold like the boxing gloves).

46 RADIO

The radio has '6' stations (and it is green like the baseball cap).

47 SEAT

The seat is shaped like a '7' (and it is brown like the book).

48 STEERING WHEEL

The steering wheel is shaped like an '8' (and it is black like the spider) so it's '48'.

49 KEY

The key is shaped like a '9' (and it is silver like the golf club) so it's '49'.

The bottle of the motor is '10'W30 (and it is white like the bowling pins). (Remember that the 10th object on each list isn't used when counting from 0 to 100, but I include it here anyway). I know; you've heard this before.

If you use 'The Car' memory palace as a stand-alone list, here are the objects and the number connections:

1. screwdriver
2. windshield
3. traffic light
4. engine
5. tire
6. stereo
7. seat
8. steering wheel
9. key
10. *oil*

Remember, you can imagine any car you want. It can be a Mustang, a Charger, a Ferrari, a Viper, or a BMW. It could even be a police car. Fair warning: they won't let you 'research' the inside, even after you tell them you're a memory expert.

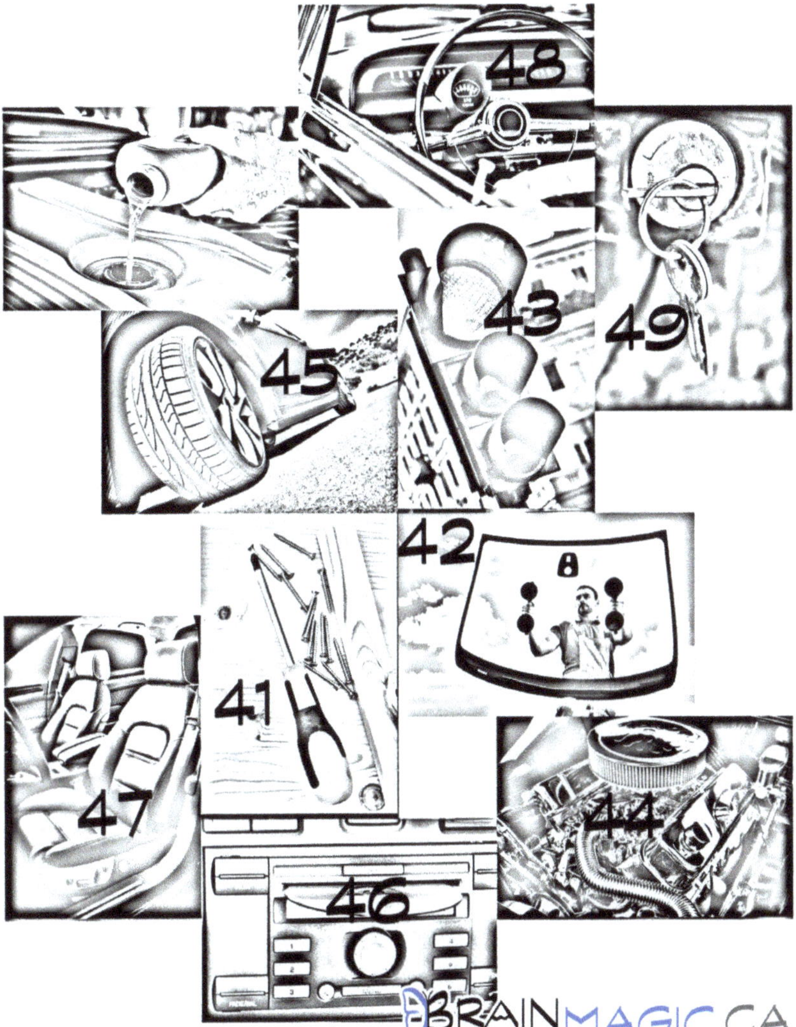

school palace

The fifth memory palace is the school.

This palace contains the numbers from 50 to 59.

50 SCHOOL BUS

The school bus is orange and has '5' sections on each wheel, so it is '50'. This will help you to remember that the car is the fifth 'memory place' and any objects in it start with '5'.

51 PENCIL

The pencil is shaped like a '1' (and it's yellow like the banana). This means that the pencil is the 51st memory hook. It is '5_' because it is from the school and '1' because it is shaped like a '1'.

52 GLOBE

A globe has '2' poles (and its oceans make it look blue like the dolphin) so it's '52'.

53 FLAG

There are '3' sections or '3' colours on the flag (and it has red like the tricycle). The Canadian flag has 3 sections. The American and Australian flags have '3' colours. Just imagine the flag you want.

(I thought about changing this one, but we're all friends).

54 LOCKER

The engine has '4' cylinders (and it is purple like the kite) so it's '54'.

55 BASKETBALL

The basketball has '5' players on each team (and it is orange like the boxing gloves) so it's '55'.

56 PENCIL SHARPENER

The pencil sharpener has '6' holes (and it's green like the baseball cap) so it's '56'.

57 PIANO

The piano has sets of '7' notes, ABCDEFG, (and it is brown like the book) so it's '57'.

58 CHESS SET

The chess set has '8' rows, '8' columns, and '8' pieces in each row (and it is 'half' black like the spider) so it's '58'.

59 SCISSORS

The scissors are shaped like two '9's (and they are silver like the golf club) so it's '59'.

The basketball hoop is shaped like a 10 from above (and the backboard is white like the bowling pins). (Remember that the 10th object on each list isn't used when counting from 0 to 100.)

If you use 'The School' memory palace as a stand-alone list, here are the objects and the number connections:

1. pencil
2. globe
3. flag
4. locker
5. basketball
6. pencil sharpener
7. piano
8. chess board
9. scissors
10. basketball hoop

You can have a pattern for each palace you create. If you use a house, then the first object in every room could be in front of the doorway. The second object could be located in the right corner of each room. The third object could be on the centre of the wall to the right. When you enter a room, you will know exactly where to look to find your objects.

SCHOOL BUS
STOP
50

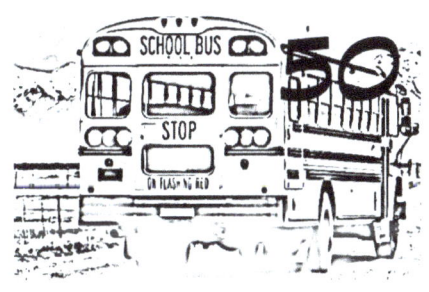

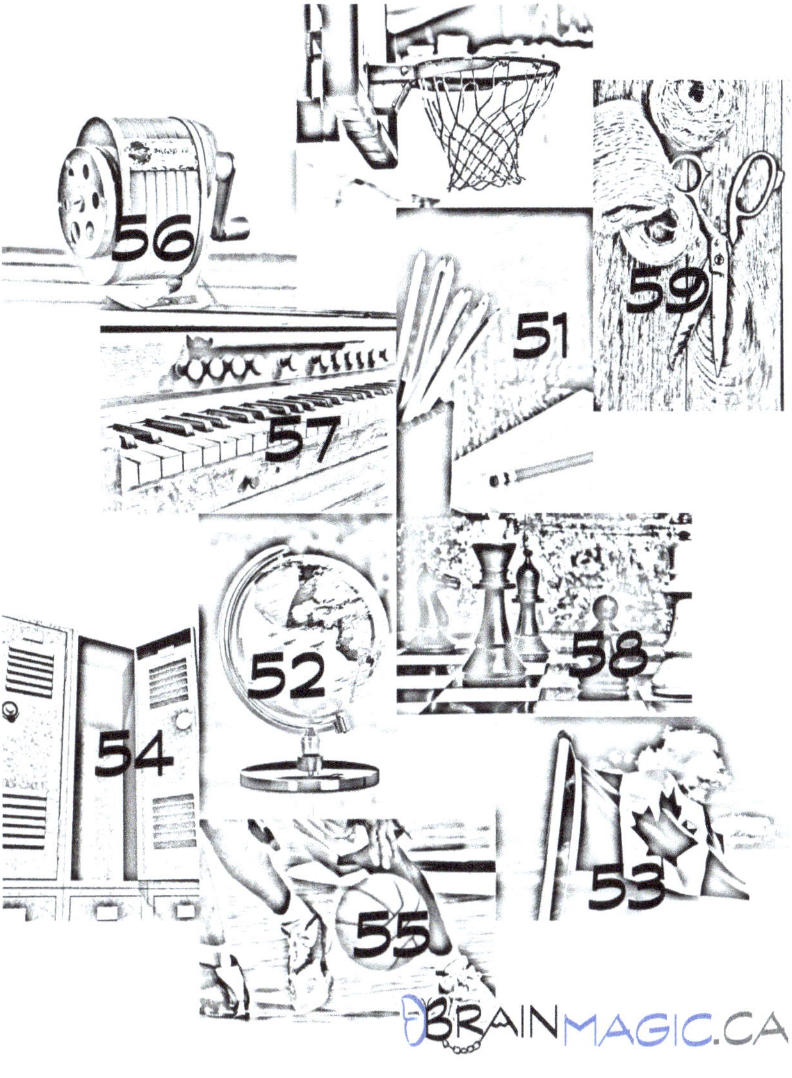
56
51
59
57
52
58
54
53
55
BRAINMAGIC.CA

farm palace

The sixth memory palace is the farm.

This palace contains the numbers from 60 to 69.

60 TRACTOR
The school bus is orange and has '5' sections on each wheel, so it is '50'. This will help you to remember that the car is the fifth 'memory place' and any objects in it start with '5'.

61 BALE
The straw bale is shaped like a '1' (and it's yellow like the banana). This means that the bale is the 61st memory hook. It is '6_' because it is from the farm and '1' because it is shaped like a '1'.

62 BLUE JAY
The blue jay has '2' wings (and it is blue like the dolphin).

63 BARREL
The barrel has '3' sections (and it is red like the tricycle).

64 PIG
The pig has '4' legs (and it is purple like the kite).

65 PITCHFORK
The pitchfork has '5' prongs (and it is orange like the boxing gloves).

66 GRASSHOPPER
The grasshopper has '6' legs (and it is green like the baseball cap).

67 COWBOY BOOT
The cowboy boot is shaped like a '7' (and it is brown like the book).

68 BULL

The bull offers '8'-second rides at the rodeo (and it is black like the spider).

69 WINDMILL

The windmill is shaped a '9' (and it is silver like the golf club).

The cowboy hat is '10', it has a band shaped like a 10, and it is white like the bowling pins. (Remember that the 10th object on each list isn't used when counting from 0 to 100.)

If you use the 'Farm' memory palace as a stand-alone list, here are the objects and the number connections:

1.	bale	6.	grasshopper
2.	blue jay	7.	cowboy boot
3.	barrel	8.	bull
4.	pig	9.	windmill
5.	pitchfork	10.	*cowboy hat*

A memory palace does not have to exist in the real world and neither do the objects inside of it. It only needs to exist inside your mind. You are the master of ... your brain things... hmmm... (I tried to think of something cool to write, but nothing came). You can imagine a room in a castle with a sword, a crown, a throne, and a stone table. It could also have a dragon, a shield, and a suit of armour. It doesn't even have to be a room. It could be a courtyard, a hilltop, or in this case a car.

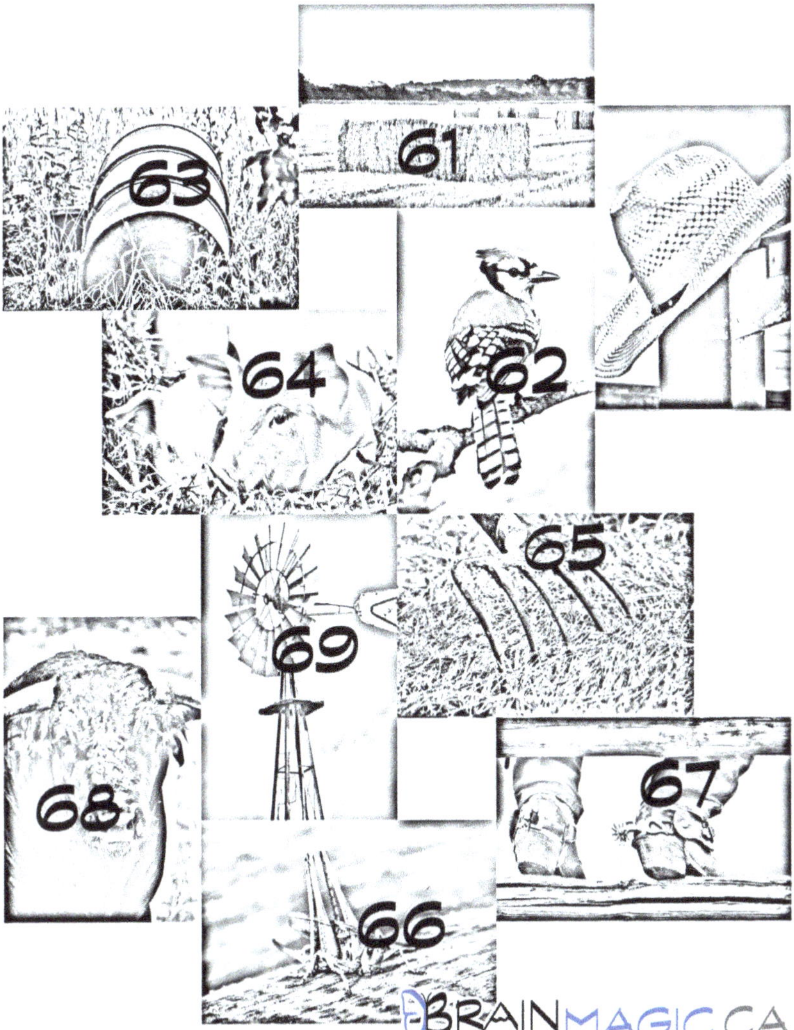

House Palace

The seventh palace is the house.

This palace contains the numbers from 70 to 79.

70 HOUSE

The house is the seventh memory palace. It has a roof shaped like the number 7 and it has '7' sections (and it is brown like a book), so it is '70'. This will help you to remember that the house is the seventh 'memory place' and any objects in it start with '7'.

71 BROOM

The broom is shaped like a '1' (and it's yellow like the banana). This means that the broom is the 71st memory hook. It is '7_' because it is from the house and '1' because it is shaped like a '1'.

72 WINDOW

The window has '2' poles (and the curtains are blue like the dolphin) so it's '72'.

73 COUCH

The couch has '3' sections (and it is red like the tricycle).

74 BED

The bed has '4' posts (and it is purple like the kite) so it's '74'.

75 CEILING FAN

The ceiling fan has '5' sections (and it is gold like the boxing gloves) so it's '75'.

76 GARDEN HOSE

The garden hose is wrapped up like a '6' (and it is green like the baseball cap) so it's '76'.

77 CLOCK

The clock hands are shaped like a '7', it runs '7' days a week, and it is brown like the book so it's '77'.

78 OUTLET

The outlet set is shaped like an '8' (and it is 'half' black like the spider) so it's '78'.

79 CAT

The cat has '9' lives (and it is grey like the golf club) so it's '79'.

The toilet is shaped like a '10' from above (and it's white like the bowling pins.) (Remember that the 10th object on each list isn't used when counting from 0 to 100.)

If you use 'The House' memory palace as a stand-alone list, here are the objects and the number connections:

1. broom	6. garden hose
2. curtains	7. clock
3. couch	8. headphones
4. bed	9. cat
5. ceiling fan	10. *toilet*

A memory palace can be any object with places to store information. People have used cupboards, bookshelves, and fridges. If you are a carpenter, a ladder can be a memory palace. You can imagine this ladder with tools positioned on or around it such as a drill, a hammer, or a saw. You could even imagine a rat underneath it as a memory hook. Now, I know what you are thinking: underneath a ladder is bad luck. In this case imagine that the rat is sitting at the top.

sports palace

The eighth memory palace is the gym.

This palace contains the numbers from 80 to 89.

80 SCORE CLOCK

The gym or sports equipment room is the eighth memory place. The score clock is the symbol for the gym. It has numbers that look like an '8' when it's off (and it is black like a book), so it is '80'. This will help you to remember that the gym is the eighth 'memory place' and any objects in it start with '8'.

81 BAT

The bat is shaped like a '1' (and it's yellow like the banana). This means that the broom is the 81st memory hook. It is '8_' because it is from the gym and '1' because it is shaped like a '1'.

82 DUMBBELL

The dumbbell has '2' sides (and it is blue like the dolphin) so it is '82'.

83 HOCKEY NET

The net looks like a '3' on top (and it is red like the tricycle).

84 SKATEBOARD

The skateboard has '4' wheels (and it is purple like the kite) so it's '84'.

85 BALL GLOVE

The glove has '5' fingers (and it is orange like the boxing gloves) so it is '85'.

86 POOL TABLE

The pool table has '6' pockets (and it's green like the baseball cap) so it is '86'.

brain magic

87 HOCKEY STICK

The hockey stick is shaped like a '7' (and it is brown like the book) so it is '87'.

88 ROLLERBLADES

The blades have '8' wheels (and they are black like the spider) so they are '88'.

89 WHISTLE

The whistle is shaped like a '9' (and it is grey like the golf club) so it is '89'.

The basketball net is shaped like a '10' from above (and it is white like the bowling pins). Remember that the 10th object on each list isn't used when counting from 0 to 100, but I include it here anyway.

If you use the 'The Sports' memory palace as a stand-alone list, here are the objects and the number connections:

1.	baseball bat	6.	pool table
2.	dumbbell	7.	hockey stick
3.	hockey net	8.	rollerblades
4.	skateboard	9.	whistle
5.	basketball	10.	*basketball net*

If you want to use these memory palaces, keep this book where you can study them on a regular basis. I don't feel like we know each well enough to discuss your bathroom habits, but there are other places you could keep it such as on your nightstand, next to the couch, on the kitchen table, or in the car for when you have a few minutes to study.

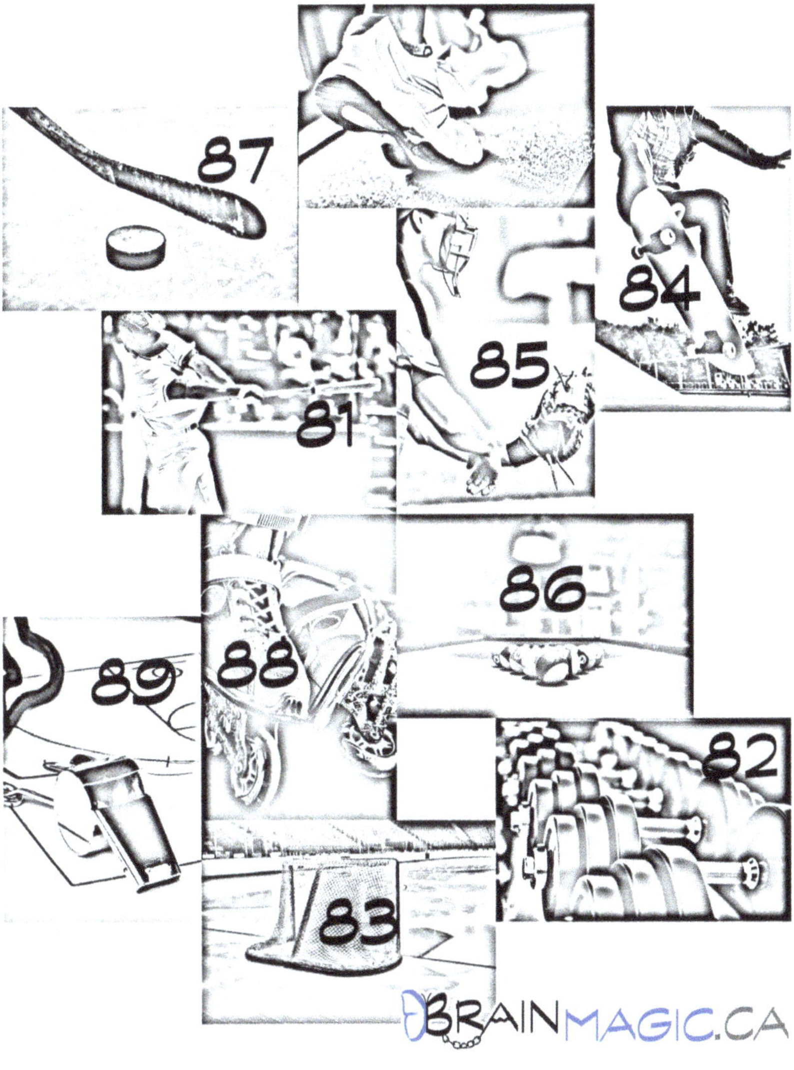

beach palace

The ninth memory palace is the beach.

This palace contains the numbers from 90 to 99.

90 SHELL

The beach is the ninth memory place. The shell is the symbol for the beach. It is shaped like a '9' (and is grey like a golf club), so it is '90'. This will help you to remember that the beach is the ninth 'memory place' and any objects in it start with '9'.

91 PADDLE

The paddle is shaped like a '1' (and it's yellow like the banana). This means that the paddle is the 91st memory hook. It is '9_' because it is from the beach and '1' because it is shaped like a '1'.

92 FLIPPERS

The flipper set has '2' flippers (and it is blue like the dolphin).

93 LIFEJACKET

The lifejacket has '3' straps (and it is red like the tricycle).

94 SAILBOAT

The sailboat has a sail shaped like a '4' (and it is purple like the kite).

95 STARFISH

The starfish has '5' sections (and it is gold like the boxing gloves).

96 TURTLE

The turtle is shaped like a '6' (and it is green like the baseball cap).

97 BOOMERANG

The boomerang is shaped like a '7' (and it is brown like the book).

98 SUNGLASSES

The sunglasses are shaped like an '8' (and they are black like the spider).

99 FISHING ROD

The fishing rod is shaped like a '9' (and it is grey like the golf club).

The snorkel and mask are shaped like a '10' (and they are white like the bowling pins). (Remember that the 10th object on each list isn't used when counting from 0 to 100.)

If you use 'The Beach' memory palace as a stand-alone list, here are the objects and number connections:

1.	paddle	6.	turtle
2.	flippers	7.	boomerang
3.	lifejacket	8.	sunglasses
4.	sailboat	9.	fishing rod
5.	starfish	10.	*snorkel and mask*

Your memory palaces should be places you like. I could spend all day in this beach palace. I would invite my cool friends (both of them), listen to music, throw the boomerang around, and just wander aimlessly across the sand. Everything in my palaces is new and awesome. If they are things you like, you are more likely to want to remember them.

90

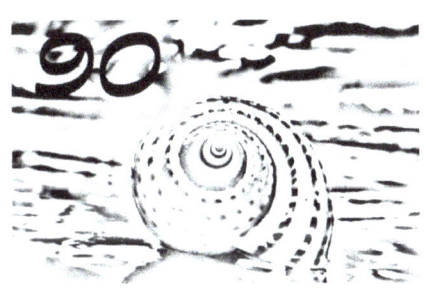

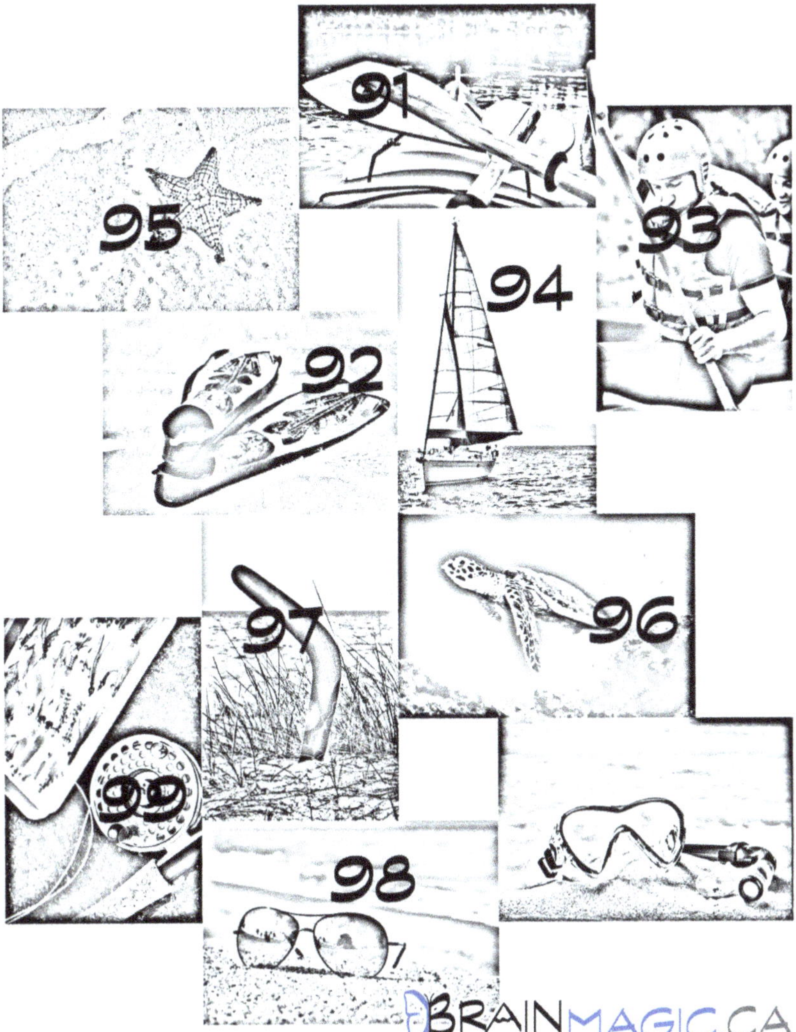
91
95
93
94
92
97
96
99
98
BRAINMAGIC.CA

Darren Mark Michalczuk

body palace

The tenth palace is the Body Palace.

The body is the tenth memory place. With the skeleton, we have all the numbers from 1 to 100. This is just an extra list that will come in handy later on.

100 SKELETON

The skeleton is the symbol for the body. It has '10' fingers and '10' toes (and it is white like the bowling pins), so it is '100'.

NOSE (1)

The nose is shaped like a '1' (and it is covered with yellow sunscreen).

REAR (2)

I would have called it the 'butt', but I'm not sure I can use that word in this book. The rear has '2' cheeks (and is covered with jeans that are blue like the dolphin).

LIPS (3)

The lips are shaped like a '3' (and they are red like the tricycle).

NECK (4)

The neck has a button pendant with '4' holes (which are purple like the kite).

HAND (5)

The hand has '5' fingers (and wears jewellery which is gold like the boxing gloves).

HAIR (6)

The hair is covered by a cap with '6' sections (which is green like … well, it is the baseball cap so this is a never-ending circle of logic).

KNEES (7)

The knees bend like a '7' (and have stains which are brown like the book).

EYES (8)

The eyes are covered by glasses which are shaped like an '8' (and they are black like the spider).

EARS (9)

The ears are shaped like a '9' (and have earrings that are silver like the golf club).

There are '10' toes (which are covered by shoes that are white like the bowling pins).

When you use the 'Body' memory palace, here are the objects and the number connections:

1.	nose	6.	hair
2.	rear	7.	knee
3.	lips	8.	eyes
4.	neck	9.	ears
5.	hand	10.	toes

I know I already put the numbers beside the body parts, but I had to make this list match the others. Some people would call this OCD, but I call it... I can't really think of anything else to call it... OK, maybe it's a little OCD. Don't judge me.

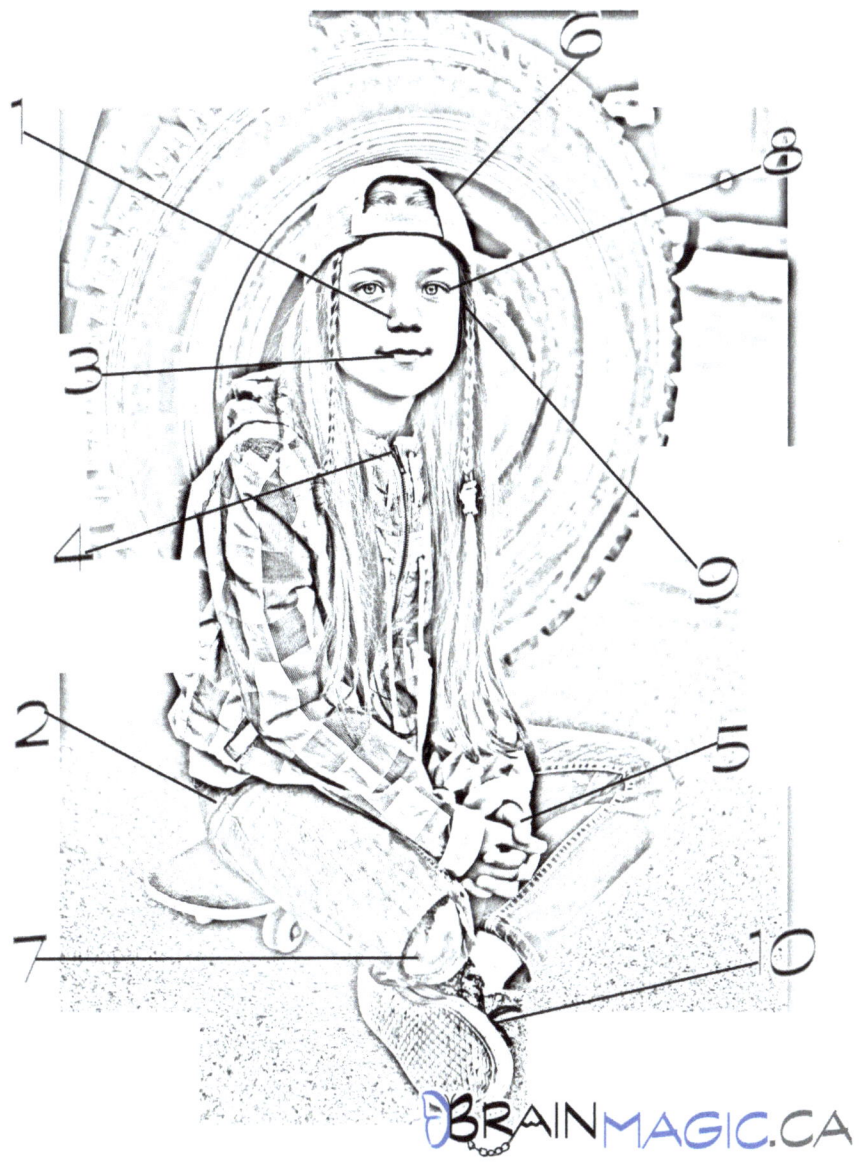

imagine the possibilities.

(The images in your palaces are like hooks, boxes, or shelves, and each one has a clearly marked number.)

Now that you've got some cool stuff in your rooms, let's play with them.

With all the cool images you have for each number up to 100, it's time to use them. You can use them like 100 numbered memory shelves to store information. One of my students used these images to remember the first 50 elements of the periodic table. The class was watching *The Lion King*, but he had already seen it. Instead of sitting through a few musical numbers performed by wild African animals, he thought he'd memorize information that most students in college chemistry classes would struggle to remember.

Though you will learn other ways to remember numbers, you can also use each object as a two-digit number. You can imagine a volleyball player on your friend's team wearing a diamond ring around her neck to remember that her jersey number is 14. You can imagine a blue jay living in your locker at school to remember that your locker number is 62. You can imagine rollerblading down a highway to remember it is Highway 88.

There are lots of numbers to memorize. As part of a writing assignment for one of my grade five classes, I had the students memorize every Academy Award-winning movie. Once the students were finished memorizing, I had them write a story based on the movie titles alone. You can imagine what they thought *Gone with the Wind* was about. Though this may not seem practical for anything other than answering questions on *Jeopardy* or other random trivia questions, it is a start to training your mind to think like a genius. Building stories using the objects from the memory palaces is something you will do over and over again as you learn to memorize information.

Academy Award-Winning Movies

Here are some movies that have won the Academy Award for Best Picture and the year they won with an example of how to remember each one. Since each year will either begin with 19__ or 20__, you only need to remember the last two digits of the year. You can use the images from the Mega Palace to remember all or just some of the items from a list. You don't have to know anything about the movie. You just have to remember the title. I'm pretty sure *Gone with the Wind* is about outlaws leaving a one-horse town after a chili-eating contest, but I could be wrong. Either way, I imagine a fan blowing leaves off a frying pan for this movie.

1965   *The Sound of Music*

Imagine a pitchfork (the image for the number '65') connected to a guitar amp (an image for 'music') while you play "The Wheels on the Bus" like a rock star. When you think of the pitchfork and this story you remember that the 1965 movie that won an Academy Award is The Sound of Music.

1995   *Braveheart*

Imagine a starfish (the image for '95') running across the sand because he stole a pendant shaped like a 'heart' for being 'brave' (the image for

'Braveheart'). When you think of the starfish and this story you will remember that the 1995 movie that won an Academy Award is Braveheart.

2004 Million Dollar Baby

Imagine a 'baby' dressed in a 'million dollars' worth of clothes and jewellery (an image for 'Million Dollar Baby') flying a 'kite' (the image for '04') in a wild windstorm. When you think of the kite and this story, you'll remember that the 2004 movie that won an Academy Award is Million Dollar Baby.

The Periodic Table Of Elements

You could also use the 'Hundred List' to memorize the elements on the periodic table, a list of all the elements that make up our world. Each element has a specific number. Students in a high school or college chemistry classes may be asked to become familiar with some of these numbers.

8   Oxygen

Imagine a spider (the image for the number '8') using an oxygen mask and tank (an image for 'oxygen') after completing a marathon. When you think of the spider and this story you will remember that the atomic or chemical number of oxygen is '8'.

20   Calcium

Imagine poking holes into a milk jug (an image for 'calcium') with a dart (the image for '20'). When you think of the dart and this story, you will remember the atomic number of calcium is '20'.

79   Gold

Image a cat (the image for '79') picking up gold coins (an image for 'gold') in an old abandoned pirate cave. When you think of the cat and this story, you will remember the atomic number of gold is '79'.

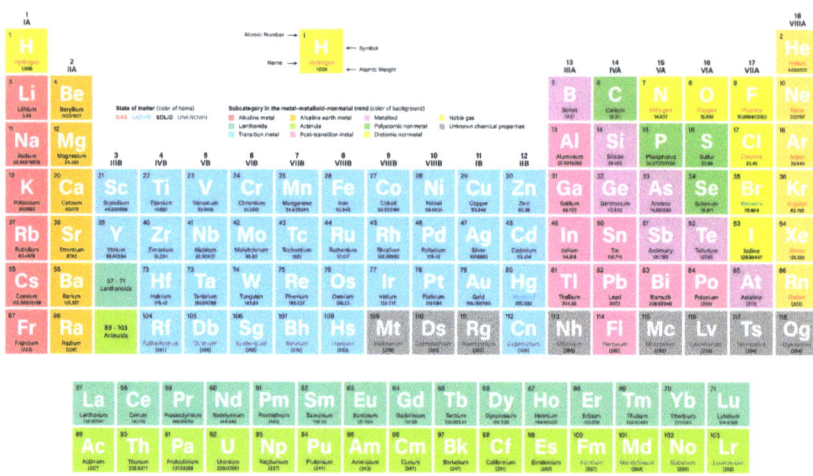

Periodic Table of the Elements

American Presidents

You could also use the 'Hundred List' to remember some history. Though you won't use all the pictures until some time past 3078, you can remember the presidents of the United States up until now. Each president has served a specific term and some, like Grover Cleveland, have served two terms in office. For example, Abraham Lincoln was the 16th president of the United States. Let's start with a lesser-known president.

11th president   James K. Polk

> Imagine a beautiful girl on a beach wearing a 'polka dot' swimsuit (an image for 'Polk') playing a game of touch football wearing a helmet (the image for '11'). When you think of the helmet and this story, you'll remember the 11th president of the United States was James K. Polk.

14th president   Franklin Pierce

Imagine Franklin the turtle wearing a giant belly button piercing (an image for 'Franklin Pierce') breaking into a bank vault to steal a diamond ring (the image for '14'). When you think of the ring and this story, you will remember that the 14th president of the United States was Franklin Pierce.

31st president   Herbert Hoover

Imagine vacuuming herbs off the carpet with a Hoover (an image for 'Herbert Hoover') in the middle of the night with a flashlight (the image for '31'). When you think of the flashlight and this story, you will remember that Herbert Hoover was the 31st president.

Darren Mark Michalczuk

birthdays

Memory Challenge

For this challenge you are going to memorize the birthday of each animal.

You have an image available for every two-digit number. Now you can also learn an image for every month as well. When you remember dates, you will use the images for the 12 months of the year over and over again. Doing this work ahead of time will increase your speed when you are given a new date to remember.

When a date includes January you can think of a giant champagne bottle, since New Year's Day comes in January. You can use this champagne bottle whether you are remembering someone's birthday, an historical date, or the date of an upcoming event. A champagne bottle can be used for anything that includes January.

Here are some images you can use for the months of the year:

January	champagne bottle	July	jewel
February	groundhog	August	autumn apple
March	toy soldiers	September	teacher desk
April	rubber boots	October	pumpkin
May	flowers	November	tank
June	June bug	December	Christmas tree

Darren Mark Michalczuk

birthdays

Cheat Sheet

Imagine:

- **Ellie** (**the tiger**) uses an **umbrella** (Apr.) to keep away an **eagle** (19).
- **Raphael** eats **eggs** (12) that have grown on a **Christmas tree** (Dec.).
- **Camille** keeps a pet **spider** (8) in a **jack o' lantern** (Oct.).
- **Jade** rides her **tricycle** (3) over a **June bug** (Jun.).
- **Andrea** decorates a **bench** (22) by gluing **autumn apples** (Aug.) on it.
- **Harper** builds a tower of **cards** (13) on a **snowman** (Feb.).
- **Graeme** puts on her **helmet** (11) and crashes into a **pumpkin** (Oct.).
- **Olivia** drives a **semi** (18) into a giant **champagne bottle** (Jan.).
- **Diane** uses **boxing gloves** (5) to gather **autumn apples** (Aug.).
- **Chris** races with a **champagne bottle** (Jan.) balanced on a **book** (7).
- **Axel** fills her **boots** (April) with **a deck of cards** (13).
- **Jess** ties a **toy soldier** (March) to a **kite** (4) she is flying.
- **Patricia** piles **autumn apples** (Aug.) over a **phone** (27).
- **Shane** places a **diamond ring** (14) on top of her **Christmas tree** (Dec.).
- **Victoria** runs over her **tent** (30) with a **tank** (Nov.)
- **Kory** washes his **pumpkin** (Oct.) near a **fire hydrant** (21).
- **Lucas** decorates a **bench** (22) with **flowers** (May.).
- **Sara** pours a **cup** (23) over a sweating **June bug** (Jun.).
- **Nora** smashes a **coffee pot** (25) over his **teacher's desk** (Sep.).
- **Aaron** puts **jewels** (July) on the wheels of his **tricycle** (3).

You've got the whole world in your hands.

(You can sing along if you feel like it. I prefer to just dance.)

If you can hold it in your hands, you can hold it in your mind.

I teach at an elementary school, so I have to find simple rules to help kids remember things. For example, when they are learning to set a volleyball, I tell them to pretend the ball is going to hit them in the forehead. This simple rule helps correct a lot of potential errors, such as footwork, body position, and shape of the hands. I coach by giving them feedback, but this simple rule is something I keep reminding them about.

One of the rules I have about memorizing is to turn each piece of information into an object. More specifically, I tell my students to turn the information into an object they can see or touch and if possible, something they can hold their hands.

If you want to remember the word moisture, thinking of water is a good start. However, this may not always be an image you can recall. If you are going to remember this as the eighth word on a list, then you would make up a story about a spider and water. Maybe you remember a spider being soaking wet. This story is ok, but you may not recall it every time. The detail of droplets of water on a spider is something you really have to focus on.

Instead of using just water, imagine something you can hold in your hands, like a watering can. A spider that is holding a watering can and sprinkling water on a flower in a garden, maybe even while wearing a sun hat and dress, will be much easier to remember than just a wet spider.

Imagining a player wearing a football helmet trying to be romantic might be a story you use to remember that the #11 word on a list is 'romantic'. Since there is no object, when you try to recall the story later on and think of the football player, you are going to have to decipher from his actions and body language what word goes with him. You might think, "Is he having a seizure? Is he being awkward? Is he a tree in a dramatic dance class?" The 'romantic' cue may not come back to you right away.

If instead you imagine the football player playing a romantic serenade with a Mexican guitar, then this will be easier to remember. The guitar is something you can see and touch, so your mind can figure out the word 'romantic' much more quickly. Also, from now on this guitar will always be your mental object for the word 'romantic' or any variation of it like 'romance' or 'romanticize'. As you create images in your mind for words, you start building a repertoire, much like you build your vocabulary as you read and learn new words. When you create an image to use for a word, you can reuse it over and over again.

The second part to the rule is to think of something you can hold with your hands that is about the size of a piece of luggage you would take on a trip. This means you will have to change most of the objects you think of, and this is a good thing. Our mind doesn't remember the ordinary; it remembers the unusual. Imagine being in kindergarten and it's "Show and Tell" day. One kid brings in a small race car toy. Most of the class yawns, stares at the ceiling, or rocks in their seat. A small race car is not something that's likely to be remembered. But the next kid brings in a rare giant ant from Uganda. It's glowing green and is the size of a full-grown Rottweiler. All of the kids are now leaning forward to get a better look. One kid asks to go to the bathroom. Another starts crying. Chances are these kids are going to remember this ant until they are in college, mainly because it is out-of-the-ordinary.

By changing the size of something you make it more memorable. If you have ever seen *Journey 2: The Mysterious Island* then you probably remember the elephants. They were small, about the size of a dog; and ever so awesome. Even the adults were looking at them like they were puppies on Christmas morning.

By changing the size of something, it instantly becomes more memorable. A water bottle that is the size of a duffle bag, a tractor that is the size of a little red wagon, or a mosquito that is the size of an end table are things that the mind will remember. It doesn't really matter if an object is bigger or smaller than usual; it just has to be the wrong size.

Make an eraser be the size of a small inflatable raft, a rollercoaster be the size of a Lego set, or a jet be the size of a sled. With practice your mind will start doing this automatically and you will be able to remember more things with less work. It's like you've got *the whole world in your hands*. Get it? It's a 'play-on-words'. Never mind. It sounded funnier in my head.

Some objects work better than others. To remember the word rain, you might think that water coming down is enough, but something that will stand out even more in your mind is an umbrella, especially if it is a colourful one with ribbons that you twirl as you go down the street singing Broadway songs. I know I'm not the only guy who does this. Come to think of it, this may be part of the reason I was never invited to parties.

The more details an object has, the more it will be a unique image that is easily recalled.

Word	**OK Image**	**Good Image**	**Great Image**
dirty:	dust	duster	vacuum
strong	chain	tractor	The Hulk
dark	shadow	ink bottle	Darth Vader
smooth	paper	floor tile	iron
wind	cloud	fan	sailboat
bounce	speed bump	ball	trampoline
up	arrow	stairs	balloons
soft	Kleenex	sponge	kitten
worth	coin	diamond	pirate chest
dry	towel	autumn leaf	hair dryer
heat	flame	campfire	torch
time	watch	alarm clock	sundial
break	stick	window	Karate Kid
flour	white flour	bag of flour	windmill
sink	rock	kitchen sink	submarine

take a number.

(You can put more than one image together, like Lego blocks of information.)

The year 1492 may seem scary, but it is just the 92nd year in the fourteen hundreds.

If numbers are more than two digits, you can simply make a story using more than one image. The last four digits of a phone number could be remembered with two images from the Mega-Palace. Numbers on a Visa credit card come in sets of four digits, which could be remembered as two images as well. City addresses, passwords, or license plates are other numbers that can be remembered by using more than one image.

The order of the images is a small detail, but can be remembered in a couple of different ways. You can have the first digit be the first image in your story. If a pig runs out of your locker and puts on rollerblades, then you can assume that the first two digits of your locker are connected to the pig (64) and the last two digits are connected to the rollerblades (88).

Like all the images you use, the more you practice them, the easier it will be to use them in your mind. You can count through the numbers from the Mega-Palace in your head as you go for a run. You can practice images for common names while you are getting ready to go to sleep. You can review the images for playing cards in the morning before you go to work or school. You can put up pictures that will help you remember the images you use frequently. I have pictures of the palaces on my fridge right next to my 'You Shouldn't Be Here' sign.

Soon you will be able to instantly think of a bull when you see the number '68', a saddle when you see the 'King of Spades', or a horseshoe when you see the last name 'Smith'.

Dial 'M' For Memory

Let's start by learning how to memorize phone numbers in a small town. All of the phone numbers in this town start with the same area code and first three numbers. For most of the phone numbers, all you really have to remember are the last four digits. Imagine the fictional town of East Spring, population 2,500, and home to a swimming pool, a three-star motel, and a seasonal museum. It also has its own casino, which some call 'just a VLT'.

Dr. Walker   780-394-4189

> *Imagine lying on the operating table and the doctor smashes the door down with his walker (an image for 'Dr. Walker'). He uses a screwdriver (the image for '41') to pry out a whistle (an image for '89') from between your toes. When you think of the doctor's room and this story, you'll remember that Dr. Walker's phone number ends with '4189'.*

Laundromat   780-394-6803

> *Imagine a small bull (an image for '68') riding a tricycle (an image for '03') into a washing machine (an image for the Laundromat). When you think of the washing machine and this story you will remember that the phone number for the Laundromat ends with '6803'.*

Penny Campbell   780-394-3354

Imagine a Campbell's soup can filled with pennies (an image for 'Penny Campbell') being carried away by a giant ant (an image for '33') into a locker (an image for '54'). When you think of Penny Campbell and this story, you will remember that her phone number ends with '3354'.

History Repeats Itself

The same method can be used to remember historical dates. You can turn the event into an image and connect that image to images that make up the date. This will put the information in a place where you can find it in your mind. Similar to having a memory palace, we can store the information in a specific place in our mind. With these examples, we will store the information in a place that reminds us of the event.

French Revolution   begins in 1789

Imagine an order of French fries on a record player (an image for the 'French Revolution') being hit by a football (an image for '17') thrown by a coach blowing a whistle (an image for '89'). When you think of the record player with French fries and this story, you will remember that the French Revolution started in 1789. If you are too young to remember record players, then just think of a giant, black CD player that spins really slowly.

Moon Landing   1969

Imagine driving a golf cart (an image for '19') across the moon (an image for the 'Moon Landing') and crashing into a windmill (an image for '69'). When you think of the moon and this story, you will remember that the 'Moon Landing' happened in 1969.

Spanish Armada Sails   1588

> *Imagine Dora the Explorer sailing a pirate ship (an image for the 'Spanish Armada') with the entire crew playing badminton (an image for '15') while wearing rollerblades (an image for '88'). When you think of Dora's ship and this story, you will remember that the Spanish Armada sailed in 1588.*

Life Numbers

This method that works for remembering important historical dates will also work for more practical tasks. Consider being a cashier at Bulk Barn, a Canadian store that sells bulk foods. Each item has a four-digit code that identifies it.

Dried Strawberries   1886

> *Imagine driving a semi (an image for '18') around a pool table (an image for '86') delivering strawberries to each one of the six pockets. When you think of strawberries and this story, you'll remember that the bin number for dried strawberries is '1886'.*

This method could also be used to remember streets and addresses.

Brian Parker   9804 Young Street

> *Imagine a giant brain (an image for 'Brian') driving a tow truck (an image for 'Parker') with a baby (an image for 'Young Street') in the passenger seat over an expensive pair of sunglasses (an image for '98') while pulling a giant kite (an image for '04'). When you think of a brain driving a tow truck and this story, you'll remember that Brian Parker lives at 9804 Young Street.*

This method could also be used to remember passcodes.

Safe Passcode   6210

Imagine that your hotel safe opens and blue jays (an image for '62') fly out carrying bowling balls (an image for '10'). When you think of the safe and this story, you'll remember that the passcode is '6210'.

Extra Digits

At times you'll need to remember a three-digit number. In this case you can add a specific quality to an image you already know.

Lightning

Any object that has lightning (a quality that is yellow like the banana) going through it will have a '1' in front of it. For example, a car (the image for '40') with lightning going through it is an image for '140'.

Underwater

Any object that is underwater (a quality that is blue like the dolphin) will have a '2' in front of it. For example, a car stereo (the image for '46') that is underwater is an image for '246'.

Fire

Any object that is on fire (a quality that is red like the tricycle) will have a '3' in front of it. For example, a piano (the image for '57') that is on fire is an image for '357'.

Paint

Any object covered in paint (a quality that is purple like the kite) will have a '4' in front of it. For example, a cat (the image for '79') is an image for '479'.

Gold

Any object that is solid gold (a quality that is gold like the boxing glove) will have a '5' in front of it. For example, a badminton birdie (the image for '15') that is solid gold is an image for '515'.

Leaves

Any object that is covered in leaves (a quality that is green like the baseball cap) will have a '6' in front of it. For example, a baseball bat (the image for '81') covered in leaves is an image for '681'.

Mud

Any object that is stuck in the mud (a quality that is brown like the book) will have a '7' in front of it. For example, a starfish (the image for '95') stuck in mud is an image for '795'.

Oil

Any object that is covered in motor oil (a quality that is black like the spider) will have an '8' in front of it. For example, a fire hydrant (the image for '21') covered in oil is an image for '821'.

Stone

Any object that is made of stone (a quality that is grey like the golf club) will have a '9' in front of it. For example, a key (the image for '49') made out of stone is an image for '949'.

Glass

Any object that is made of glass (a quality that is clear like 'nothing') will have a '0' in front of it. For example, a ring (the image for '14') made of glass is an image for '014'.

Here is a quick reference list of these qualities:

0	glass	5	gold
1	lightning	6	leaves
2	underwater	7	mud
3	fire	8	oil
4	paint	9	stone

You can combine these images to make larger numbers connected with images of your choice. Other things you can memorize with these images are numbers from credit cards, key pages, license plates, or birth dates. Now you have the images to use to remember any number. How cool is that?

Area Codes

Sometimes you may want to remember three-digit numbers. Area codes would be one example of this. For each place you can create an object to use in your mind to make it easier to remember. The object can come from the name, a landmark from the area, or just be something that pops into your head when you think of the place. Here are some examples of how to remember area codes:

Los Angeles   Area Code 213

Imagine a lost angel playing cards underwater. The lost angel will help you remember Los Angeles. Being underwater will help you remember that the first digit of the area code is '2'. The cards will help you remember that the last two digits of the area code are 13. This is an image that will help you remember that Los Angeles' area code is 213.

Nunavut   Area Code 867

Imagine walking through Canada's north holding hands with a polar bear that is wearing cowboy boots covered in oil. The polar bear will remind you of the northern province of Nunavut. The oil will remind you that the first digit is 8. The cowboy boots will remind you that the last two digits are 67. This is an image that will help you remember that Nunavut's area code is 867.

Phoenix   Area Code 480

Imagine a phoenix trying to change the score on a score clock covered in paint. The phoenix is a symbol for the city of Phoenix (Arizona). Paint is an object for the first digit '4'. A score clock is an object for the number '80'. This simple image will help you remember that the area code for Phoenix is 480.

Phone Numbers

Memory Challenge

For this challenge you are going to memorize local phone numbers in a small town where the area code is always the same.

To remember these phone numbers, start by changing each business into an image of an object you see or touch. Thinking of a bank as a building is ok, but it can easily be confused with a courthouse or a school. Thinking of a bank as a piggy bank makes it easier to keep it separate from the other businesses. Having an object will also make it easier to make a simple, memorable story to lock in the information.

Here are some images you can use for each place:

bank	piggy bank	groceries	basket
train station	train	music	record
library	book shelf	health store	vitamins
photo lab	camera	emergency	ambulance
dairy shop	ice cream cone	marina	boat
rec centre	tennis racket	post office	letter
digital store	iPad	tow services	tow truck
bike shop	bike	bottle depot	bottle
art studio	palette	medical lab	microscope
waste	garbage can	lounge	glass

City Bank 635-9784	Central Train Station 835-1209	Public Library 933-2751	One Hour Photo Lab 227-2098

Ice Cream Shop 848-2463	Recreation Centre 582-2879	Electronics Store 218-3764	Bike Repair 288-2957

Art Studio 763-2187	Waste Disposal 567-3301	Market Groceries 953-2235	Mark's Music 209-0024

Health Foods 635-9784	Grey Nun's Emergency 285-0804	West Coast Marina 287-2653	Main Street Post Office 230-1910

County Tow Services 665-6133	Bottle Depot 286-7984	East Valley Medical Lab 345-1692	Danny's Lounge 231-3476

Phone Number

Cheat Sheet

Imagine:

- A **piggy bank** throws a **boomerang** (97) at a **skateboarder** (84).
- A toy **train** hauls **eggs** (12) travelling over tracks made of **golf clubs** (09).
- A **pencil** (51) pushes over a **book shelf** onto a **phone booth** (27).
- A **dart** (20) shot from a **camera** at a pair of **sunglasses** (98).
- An **ice cream cone** in a **barrel** (63) rolled into a **baby stroller** (24).
- A **racket** hitting tennis balls at a **cat** (79) with an **umbrella** (28).
- A **pig** (64) chops up an **iPad** in a store with an **ax** (37).
- A **bike** (20) is pulling an **umbrella** (28) carrying a **chess knight** (57).
- An artist scrapes the paint off a **palette** with a **hockey stick** (87) and rinses it with water from a **hydrant** (21).
- Out of a **trash can** some **ants** (33) are carrying a **banana peel** (01).
- A **basket** full of baby **pigs** (64) is dumped onto the keys of a **piano** (57).
- Use a **record** to flip a **baseball** (00) into a **baby stroller** (24).
- Pour out a **vitamin bottle** onto a **chess board** (58) that is balanced on a **skateboard** (84).
- An **ambulance** is chasing after a **spider** (08) that is flying a **kite** (04).
- On a **yacht** (bank) some little **army men** (26) are holding a **flag** (53).
- Out of an **envelope** flies an **eagle** (19) carrying a **bowling ball** (10).
- Inside a **plastic bottle** a **cat** (79) is **skateboarding** (84).
- Under a **microscope** a **frog** (16) is swimming around with **flippers** (92).
- Inside a **glass** some **butterflies** (34) drink from a **water hose** (76).

brain magic

Post Office	Train Station	Library	Photo Lab

Ice Cream Shop	Rec Center	Electronics Store	Bike Shop

Art Studio	Waste Disposal	Grocery Store	Music Store

Health Foods	Ambulance	Marina	Post Office

Tow Truck	Bottle Depot	Medical Lab	Lounge

Darren Mark Michalczuk

Go Ahead. Make Some Memories. I Dare You.

(When you make good memories, you'll want to visit them again.)

You can become like a movie director, creating great memories in your mind.

Some things we remember more clearly than others. We remember things like weddings, car accidents, movie scenes, and first dates. There are reasons why we remember some things and not others. If we understand what makes a good memory, then we can create specific memories to hold information that will last.

The details you include in your stories will be different depending on whether you want to remember something short term or for a long time. In memory competitions you only have a certain amount of time to memorize items, and the faster you can do so, the higher your score.

Some groups put on memory competitions either online or in specific cities. These events are roughly the same in that competitors are asked to memorize information in a set amount of time. For most of these competitions, such as one put on by the Memory League, you are asked to memorize a deck of cards as quickly as possible. To remember information like this that I will only need to remember for a few minutes. I might imagine as story such as a bear (my image for the Jack of Hearts) biting my toes (the 10th place on the Body Palace). I don't care why he is there, what colour his eyes are, or what kind of mood he is in. I just simply imagine a bear biting my toes. No deep meaning.

For things that I want to remember for a long time, I would take more time to lock in the story. If I met an old friend from school who now has a child named 'Simon', I would make up a story that I could remember for a long time so that the next time we met I would still remember his son's name. I would imagine my friend playing the game 'Simon' (with the four-coloured buttons) at his parents' cabin. I would imagine beating him so bad that he cried, or maybe I would imagine playing 'Simon' on the roof of his parents' cabin where the hummingbirds feed. The more details you add to a story, the more likely you are to remember it.

Weirdness

As you learn to connect objects with simple stories or images, you will start to imagine things that wouldn't happen in everyday life. This is a good thing since your mind will go back to things that are out of the ordinary. If it doesn't make sense, then you will go back to it again and again. If you have eggs for breakfast, a year from now you probably won't remember if it was eggs, cereal, toast, or pancakes. However, if you have something that you don't normally have (like raw fish eyes), then you will probably remember it.

Imagine listening to a child in kindergarten who is telling you about her day. If she told you that she had made an 'animal' craft with construction paper and glue, Billy Thompson had gotten in trouble for fighting during a soccer game, and she had Animal Crackers for afternoon snack, then you might think that she had a pretty ordinary day. You probably wouldn't think about it much afterwards. You were just being polite by listening to her but you really wanted to get back to checking your phone.

However, if she told you that during art class an elephant had gotten loose from a circus truck passing through town, come into the classroom through the east wall, picked up Billy Thompson and dunked him in the aquarium, then you might have a different reaction. You might stare at the child for a few seconds while you tried to make sense of the story, and then you might ask her if that really happened. After double-checking the story with the teacher, you might tell this story to the first person you see, maybe your mother or at least your close friends on Facebook. It is definitely something you would remember for a long time, maybe even long enough to tell your high school crush at your next high school reunion. Out-of-the-ordinary is something that you will remember. If you want to have a strong mind, then create weird stories in your mind - the weirder, the better. Story of my life.

Emotions

I tell a story in my math class to help students remember what 6 x 7 is. The basic story is that one student is wearing a baseball cap (6) while another student stacks books (7) on it. The tower of books becomes so high that it falls and breaks the windshield of a car (42). When I go to different classes to teach this story to other students, I try and make the story more memorable for them.

One way to make a story more memorable is to trigger an emotion. I tell them that the car is the principal's car to trigger the 'OMG' emotion. I also tell them that it was his brand new Ford Mustang that he special-ordered from some random country. The more they feel when I tell the story, the more they will remember. I generally stay away from fear, as I don't want the memories to be traumatic. I do, however, try to trigger other emotions like happiness, excitement, or pride.

Of course, one of the best emotions to trigger is joy. If something makes you smile, laugh, or feel good, then you are going to want to think about again. If I tell this story to younger students, then I make sure I use my best goofy voice, dance around while pretending to stop the books from falling off my cap, and appear dumbfounded while looking at the smashed windshield. Think of things that make you laugh, and the memories will stick.

There are lots of ways to trigger your emotions. Use your favourite ball cap, steal gold coins from your brother, or pour cream over your boss's car. Just make sure you can handle the guilt. I once imagined asking my son's teacher to go watch a boxing match between two pumpkins to remember when World Teacher Day was. To this day, I feel so embarrassed that I can't go into her classroom. I just send a cardboard figure of John Stamos to the parent/teacher interviews.

Senses

Another way to make a memory story more memorable is to make sure to involve as many senses as possible. For example, if you are memorizing a list of words and the seventh word on the list is 'hummingbird', you might think of these birds flying out of the pages of a book. As you see this in your mind you could focus on the sound of their wings and the colours of their feathers. You could also imagine hundreds of hummingbirds of all different colours like red, green, purple, orange, and yellow, each with a unique flight pattern to give your mind more to pay attention to.

As you learn to connect objects with stories, you will learn to make them 'stick' in your mind with more details. Recalling the smell and taste of a lemon, the soft touch of a blanket, the intricate texture of a stone on the wall of a castle, or the familiar hum of a car engine are all ways of focusing your mind on the details. These details will give your mind more to look for and find when you look for things you want to remember.

Students in school are often taught to walk in straight lines, staring forward and keeping their hands to themselves. To build a strong memory, just the opposite should be done. As you walk you should take a look around at the world. See the bright colours in plants, smell the rain, or feel the wind. Pay attention to patterns on fabric and feel the texture of materials like wood, steel, or cement.

The more you take in the details of things, the more you will be able to recreate them in your mind. The shape, colour, and size of objects become clearer as you pay attention to details. To be able to imagine a lemon in your mind, you should first hold one in your hand. Breathe in the fresh scent, see the bright yellow colour, and taste the sourness. Be one with the universe, just like Yoda said. Or maybe it was Kermit the Frog. I can't remember.

i offer a thousand pardons.

(People often ask how much work it will take, but don't want to hear the answer.)

To become good at making one free throw, a player needs to practice a thousand times.

One thousand is an amount that is sometimes used to express a large idea. A picture is worth a thousand words. One thousand origami cranes hold special meaning in Japanese culture. "A Thousand Years" is a song by Christina Perri that many people choose for the first song at a wedding reception. It's also a good number to use as a benchmark for learning. Although every learner is different, people often want to have an idea of how long it should take to learn something new. One thousand hours is a number that will help. It's probably not the number you were hoping for, but it's a practical one. Some believe it takes ten thousand hours to master a skill, but one thousand hours is at least a solid start .

When I first learned to play piano, it was on an electronic keyboard that I had picked up at a department store. The song was "Let It Be" by the Beatles and people were impressed that I had learned it in just a few days. I have to admit that I did play it well. It wasn't just simple chording patterns or just one part of the song. It was the entire song including the harmonies, chorus, bridge sections, and solos.

The part that most people don't understand is that I spent every hour that I was awake practicing this song. It was one of the demo songs that I could see played by the keys lighting up. I could slow it down and play it over and over again until I could mimic the patterns. Although I could replicate the sound of the song, I in no way understood music. It would take some time to truly understand melodies, harmonies, chords, tempos, and key signatures.

There are people who can plunk out melodies of songs they have heard, even ones they have only heard once. Some believe this to be a sign of a gifted musician. But in reality music is much more than repeating a few notes.

Learning to read music, play with other musicians, or be creative with songs takes time. After practicing a song a thousand times, playing will be more of a skill rather than something you have to think about. Take a folk song like "Simple Gifts". If you are not familiar with it, imagine an upbeat song with a range of about 10 notes that takes about a minute to play. If a child practices three times a week for 20 minutes, this song could be played roughly 50 times each week. Though the song would be slow and choppy for the first few weeks, by week 20 it would sound like it was being played by a professional musician.

I give the number one thousand to help people, especially children, understand that skill takes work. Though memory skills make things faster, they still need to be practiced. Some professional golfers are said to swing a new club a thousand times before making a decision on purchasing it. Professional basketball and hockey players practice a shot a thousand times. A professional musician will practice playing songs a thousand times before performing. It makes sense.

Many coaches will say to practice, not until you get it right, but until you can't get it wrong. There is a huge difference between these two things. Imagine making a putt on a golf green. If you stopped at the first shot you made, then you wouldn't be very good. If you practiced until you could make a shot every time, whether it was against the wind, on wet grass, or while a crowd was making noise, then you would have skill.

Using memory skills to remember the names of a few co-workers, family members, or teammates means that you know how to use the techniques. Practicing until you can remember the names and faces of 20 strangers in one minute means you are developing a skill. The same can be said for memorizing cards, numbers, or images.

People who take memorizing seriously make these techniques a part of their daily routine. Alex Mullen from the United States, Marwin Wallonius from Sweden, and Katie Kermode from England are some of the 'memory athletes' who compete in memory competitions. They develop strategies for each event such as creating an image for each card in a deck or a memory palace to store information. They train to be able to do these skills quickly. This may mean improving their strategy with small changes. Using a sharp, black rock for the two of spades may not be working so it may be exchanged for a sea turtle instead.

These memory athletes can memorize the order of a deck of cards in less than 30 seconds, a string of 100+ numbers in less than one minute, and the first and last names of 40+ people (including names like Ektoros Panagiotis, Aleksandr Bagirov, or Cristea Pongratz).

They may find faster ways to store information. One method labelled the 'PAO' system that is commonly used for memorizing cards or numbers allows someone to store three pieces of information in one place with a person-action-object pattern. An example of this might be a dolphin trainer (a person for the two of hearts) pounds some nails (an action for the ten of spades) into a bell (the object for the five of spades). This one image or story holds three cards instead of just one. This means finding a person, action, and object for each one of the 52 cards in a deck. It definitely takes some work, but that's what it takes to have a great memory.

To develop a strong memory, it takes work.

Some ways you can train your brain... wait a second, that rhymes. Give me a second to take enjoyment of my accidental play on words... ok, I'm done. I forgot what I was saying...

Oh yeah. Train your brain. It still sounds awesome.

Hang pictures of your memory palaces in places you frequent. I think the bathroom is going a little far, but maybe in the kitchen, living room, or hallway would be good places.

Review the images for things like numbers, names, or cards whenever you have a few minutes to kill. I get tons of studying done when people say, "Can you give me a minute?"

Set time aside to study. You need time to go through your images, time yourself for challenges, chart your progress, or simply practice your memory skills in a quiet setting. Don't do it in church, though. Apparently, this is frowned upon. Again, hard lessons.

Allow yourself to really get in touch with objects in your world. Feel the rough edges of tree bark or the texture on cement, notice the smell of summer rain or wax crayons, watch the colours of a setting sun or flowing stream, or listen to the sounds of a busy sidewalk or sleeping grizzly. The more you awaken your senses, the more you can create clear images to remember (and the better you'll get at avoiding predators.)

Connect with people who are willing to share their thoughts on memory. There was a time I thought I was the only one, but these people are out there. Some have brilliant ideas on memory, but some make you wonder how they have managed to stay out of prison and function in society.

i have a special card for you.

(The difference between the eight of spades and nine of clubs is about the same as the difference between a violin and a fiddle.)

**Though all the kids bring the same lunches,
they all have different lunchboxes.**

When I first learned about memory competitions, I noticed that all of them had one common event: memorizing cards. In fact, at times it is the only event. I also thought there was no way I could teach this to elementary kids without parents thinking I was training them to win at Vegas. I'm sure many of them would have already seen *Rain Man* and would assume my worst intentions.

Now the movie *21* with Kevin Spacey actually shows you how to 'count' cards, which is a technique that is completely different than memorizing cards. Memorizing cards means being able to recall the order of a deck of cards. For example, after looking through a deck of cards you will able to list them off in order (A♥, 10♠, 8♦, 9♣...). Let's try and keep this a family show.

At first I wondered why card memorization was always an event, but after I thought about it, it made sense. It is something that is easy to measure. After five minutes of memorizing, it is easy to see who has remembered more cards. It is a standard event that will be the same year after year. For events like memorizing words, one year might have more difficult words than another, making it tough to compare scores from different competitions. It's also an easy event to set up. Instead of coming up with hundreds of different words, find photos of people and assign them unique names, or research historical dates for competitors to memorize, all that is really needed is to shuffle a deck.

Before you learn to memorize with images, try remembering these eight cards by rote. Give yourself one minute, which should be plenty of time.

Chances are, you didn't remember them all and it was a lot of work to get even six correct. It would seem impossible to remember all 52 using this same method.

Here you will learn to memorize cards using images. Learning to memorize a deck has other benefits as well. As you practice remembering the order of a deck, your mind will get better at seeing things as images. It also forces you to make unique images for similar things, which is one of the keys to a powerful mind. It's like jogging to improve your fitness, but in this case you are exercising your mind.

As with other information, the best way to remember cards is to think of objects. When you turn each card into an image, then you have something that your mind will be able to find easily. The numbers, shapes, and colours of the cards will blend together unless we see each one as an image that is very unique.

It's like all the kids at school having a sandwich, a piece of fruit, and a juice box for lunch. Trying to tell these lunches apart would be a nightmare in a class of 52 kids. But if each child had a different lunchbox, then it would be easy. Jamie would look for his red Ironman lunchbox, Beth would look for her Smurf one, and Melissa is the first to find her Justin Bieber box. Melissa often eats alone in the cafeteria.

In the mind the face of an eight of hearts card will look very similar to a nine of diamonds card. However, a saddle, a spider web, an airplane, and a church bell all look very different. If you can see each card as an object, it will be easy to keep them separate and to place them in a memory palace in your mind.

To remember the suits, each object has a general shape.

Suits

- ♣ Clubs are objects that are round.
- ♥ Hearts are objects that are red and heart-shaped.
- ♠ Spades are objects that are pointed.
- ♦ Diamonds are white objects that are diamond-shaped.

These shapes will help you remember the suit when you think of an image. An iceberg has the shape of a diamond. Boxing gloves are shaped like a heart when you hold them together. A spider has pointed legs so it's a spade. A yo-yo is round, so it's a club.

For the numbers, I use objects from the 'Kids Palace'; and for the letters, I use objects that make sense to me.

A	Aces are things that fly like a "flying ace".
2	2's are things in the ocean like a 'dolphin'.
3	3's are things from a 'tricycle'.
4	4's are toys on a string like the 'kite'.
5	5's are boxing things.
6	6's are baseball things.
7	7's are writing things.
8	8's are spider things.
9	9's are golf things.
10	10's are bowling things.
J	J's are fishing things like a 'Jackfish'.
Q	Q's are bee things like a 'queen bee'.
K	K's are king things.

The object for each card will help you remember both the suit and number or letter. The five of hearts will be something from boxing (since the boxing glove is '5') and is shaped like a heart, so the pair of boxing gloves is the five of hearts. The iceberg is from the ocean (like a dolphin which is the image for '2') and is shaped like a diamond, so it is the image for the two of diamonds. A spider (the image for '8') has pointed legs (the shape for spades) so it is the eight of spades. The bowling ball (the image for '10') is round so it is the ten of clubs.

To make objects work better in the mind, some are exaggerated. The tricycle things are good examples of this. The seat of the tricycle is exaggerated into a big, bouncy red dodgeball. It has more possibilities for creating good memories than just a seat. The basket is an Easter basket. The screw becomes a giant drill. The wheel is a large tire from a monster truck. These are all made bigger or cooler so that they are easier to build memories with.

For some of the objects, once you make the connection you'll remember every time after that. Think of using a bandana to clean golf balls or a spider catching a housefly. A shovel can be used to keep the grounds on a baseball field. A black hole is just a 'super' version of the hole on a golf green. Once your mind makes sense of something, it is easy to remember.

The best way to practice these images is to flip through a deck of cards. As you see each card you should be able to see the image that goes with it. One card every second is a good goal to reach, which means you should be able to go through a deck in about a minute. Think of each card being a flashcard. It will help you relive the days of elementary school. Memories of being scared to ask to go to the bathroom, hiding in the corner during dodgeball, and trying to put your tongue on frozen metal will come flooding back. I know I'm not the only one who tried the tongue thing.

Hearts (♥'s):

A♥ parachute	2♥ dolphin	3♥ dodgeball
4♥ balloon	5♥ boxing gloves	6♥ ball glove
7♥ candy box	8♥ housefly	9♥ bandana
10♥ trophy		
J♥ fish	Q♥ honey jar	K♥ saddle

Spades (♠'s):

A♠ arrow	2♠ turtle	3♠ drill
4♠ top	5♠ chair	6♠ shovel
7♠ pen	8♠ spider	9♠ flag pole
10♠ spray can		
J♠ spear gun	Q♠ mosquito	K♠ sword

Diamonds (♦'s):

A♦ plane	2♦ iceberg	3♦ basket
4♦ kite	5♦ whip	6♦ base
7♦ envelope	8♦ web	9♦ eagle
10♦ bowling pins		
J♦ boat	Q♦ hive	K♦ princess

Clubs (♣'s):

A♣ UFO	2♣ submarine	3♣ wheel
4♣ yo-yo	5♣ bell	6♣ baseball
7♣ ink bottle	8♣ spider eggs	9♣ hole
10♣ bowling ball		
J♣ fish hook	Q♣ queen bee	K♣ shield

After you have memorized the image for each card, the next step is to remember them in order. There are a few ways you can do this. You can try to place each card into a specific place in your memory palace or make a memory journey by connecting each card to the next.

To start, you can remember the cards by using a memory story that connects the images for each card. Remember, the story doesn't have to make perfect sense; it just has to be memorable. This will help you to remember more cards, but if you forget one card, you won't be able to remember any after this. Though this method isn't perfect, it is a place to start.

Imagine this:

> *A UFO (ace of spades) uses a beam to pick up a giant trophy (ten of hearts) and throw it a mosquito (queen of spades). The mosquito takes a flagpole (nine of spades) and jabs at a bowling ball (ten of clubs). The ball starts rolling down*

a hill and crashes into a boat (jack of diamonds). On impact, it releases 99 red balloons (four of hearts ... and a pretty cool 80s song) into the air and ...

Another similar way to memorize is to use a technique called 'chaining' or 'linking'. It's like creating a memory journey but with several smaller stories, like links in a chain. Again, it doesn't leave room for mistakes.

Imagine a UFO destroying a giant trophy with a beam. This will connect the ace of spades to the ten of hearts.

Imagine a trophy being attacked by a swarm of mosquitoes. This will connect the ten of hearts to the queen of spades.

Imagine a mosquito throwing a flagpole like a javelin into the woods. This will connect the queen of spades to the nine of spades.

Imagine hitting a bowling ball with a flagpole like you are in the middle of a World Series baseball game. This will connect the nine of spades to the ten of clubs.

In memory competitions these methods wouldn't be effective because the stress and time pressure would cause you to forget at least one card, leaving you stuck for the rest. It would, however, be great to show some kids a magic trick. Once you have the order of a deck memorized, you can ask a child to pick one card. You can even let him cut the deck once or even several times as it won't change the order. After a card is picked you simply glance at the bottom card from where it was chosen. Since you know the order, you will know what the next card is.

I'm sure you can get creative and make it more of a show with smoke, mirrors, and maybe even a giant tiger. When you say 'abracadabra' and dramatically reveal the name of the card, the children will be amazed. Unless they are too old for magic. Then you are just standing there awkwardly with a crayon drawing of the queen of spades on your forehead. Suddenly you don't get invited to family birthday parties and you become that 'weird uncle who probably doesn't have a job'.

The most effective method is to place each card (or set of cards) into a memory place. If you use your 'mega palace', you have 100 places to put information - but you will only need 52. Since the cards are based on the 'Kids' List', you can replace it with the 'Body List'. This will keep you from getting images confused. This means that instead of the first memory place being the banana, it will be your nose. Instead of the eighth place being the spider (since spider will be use for the eight of spades), use your eyes.

To remember the first card, imagine a UFO (the image for the ace of clubs) flying out of your nose (the first image on the body list).

To remember the fifth card, imagine a bowling ball (the image for the ten of clubs) falling from the sky and landing on your hand (the fifth thing on the body list).

To remember the 18th card, imagine a semi (the image for '18') being driven wildly by a spider (the image for eight of spades).

To remember the 42nd card, imagine a sword (the image for the king of spades) slashing through the windshield of the car (the image for '42').

You could put two cards in one place, but this does take practice. For example you could imagine a boat (Jack of diamonds) carrying a load of letters (seven of diamonds) and crashing into a fire hydrant (21).

Each object can have a person attached to it, such as a knight holding a sword or Spiderman spinning a web. This will give your mind more to hold on to.

As you practice memorizing cards, you will be able to make the images bigger and clearer and the connections stronger and more memorable. These skills will transfer to memorizing other things.

I was going to make a challenge for memorizing cards, but it's a lot of work. I'd have to find the graphics for each card, resize each one to fit in a grid that would fit 52 cards, rearrange them so that they are all out-of-order, and then figure out a way to make a blank page for recall. Really? Do I have to do everything for you people?

Just grab a deck of cards and shuffle them. If you want to be really official, have someone else lay them face-up on a table for you.

A word is worth a thousand pictures.

(A journey of a thousand miles begins with a single step, but so does a walk to the bathroom.)

You can build a large vocabulary, one word at a time like you can build a princess castle, one Lego block at a time.

Learning to remember what words mean is something that can be done with the skills you have already been practicing. The basic method that is taught throughout this book is to turn information into things or images and connect them with a story. I'd love to make it sound more complex and sophisticated, but it's really that simple.

With words you turn the word into an object and the definition into an object and then you connect the two objects in your mind. The objects should be things you can see or touch. A word can be a combination of two or more objects like a 'unicorn riding a tricycle' for the word 'tricorn'. The objects should be unique and easily recognized in the mind. If you are trying to remember the word 'record', a document on a clipboard is going to be too boring. Instead, one of Elvis Presley's platinum records would work much better. If you are too young to remember Elvis, then try one by Michael Jackson. If you are too young for Michael try Justin Bieber. If you don't like Justin, do some research on Elvis or The Beatles.

Turning words into images will take some practice, but you will get better at it. You find an image that rhymes (like a snowshoe hare for the word 'heir'), that makes up the smaller parts of a word (like a hippo wearing a campus jacket for 'hippocampus'), or simply a word that makes you think of the word (like an apple for the word 'gravity'). Choose images that your mind will be able to hang on to.

You can do the same thing with definitions. Often definitions are way too long when a simpler definition will work. For the word 'cedar' the online definition says *'any of a number of conifers that typically yield fragrant, durable timber, in particular'*. Instead, you could simply think of a cedar as 'a tree with needles'. Just because you use more words doesn't necessarily mean you know more. Those dictionary guys are such showoffs.

I'm sure you get the gist of this, so let's take a look at some examples.

coniferous:

> a tree that bears cones and evergreen needle-like or scale-like leaves.
>
> *Imagine a group of rowdy teenage evergreen trees going for a ride on a Ferris wheel and having a fight with ice cream cones.*

(Coniferous (cone+ferris) means evergreen tree.)

hypothermic:

> the condition of having an abnormally low body temperature, typically one that is dangerously low.
>
> *Imagine a hippo pouring a thermos of hot soup over a snowman's head.*

(Hypothermic (hippo+thermos) means being really cold.)

scarcity

> The condition in which economic wants for goods and services are greater than the limited resources available to satisfy those wants.
>
> *Imagine running through the streets of a city with the last Elmo doll on Christmas Eve and an angry crowd wearing scary Scream masks is chasing you.*

(Scarcity (scare+city) means there's not enough.)

You can make the images more complex if there is more information that you need to remember. If it is an animal you want to define, then you could make up a story like this one:

Polar bear

> *Imagine a polar bear holding a spray can of black paint in his right arm. His left arm is in a cast, but he's holding a see-through fur coat. He has a tattoo of a snowflake in a circle on his left cheek. He is chasing after 'Mary' from 'Mary had a Little Lamb' because she stole his watch. He drops his wallet, which has fifteen one hundred dollar bills folded to look like a badminton birdie because he was going to buy some meat from the market.*

Now this story reminds me that the bear has black skin (from the paint can) and clear fur (from the see-through coat). He is left-handed (from the cast) and lives in the Arctic Circle (from the tattoo). His name means 'Maritime' bear (from Mary with the timepiece) and he can weigh up to fifteen hundred pounds.

The same method could be used to define a person, so to speak. This story tells about one of the prime ministers of Australia:

Andrew Fisher

Imagine a fisherman coming out of his house, which is a church with a giant cross on the roof. He walks into a coal mine and gives all of the miners picket signs. On a 'naughty' list he blacks out everyone's name with a permanent marker. Someone throws a giant dime at him and tells him to get out, twice. He goes outside and hops onto a goose that migrates down to a chessboard where they crash into the white queen.

This story will help you remember some information about Andrew Fisher, an Australian prime minister. Read the story again and notice details that will help you remember these memories of his early life:

Andrew Fisher grew up in Crosshouse and at the age of ten started working in a coal mine. He twice led miners to strike for a 10% wage increase but was fired twice; the second time he was also blacklisted. Later he migrated to Queensland to look for other work.

Obviously there is more to Andrew Fisher's life, but this is a start. To remember more about him, you can simply continue making a memory journey that includes details about his life. Notice that we continue using objects to give our mind something to hold onto, like the dime for '10%', the permanent marker for the 'blacklist', and the white queen for 'Queensland'. We can even go back and add to our stories to include more details as time goes on.

Whatever you want to define, whether it's a word, a person, a place, a thing, or an idea, having one image as an anchor will allow you to connect information to it with images. For learning about the polar bear, a bear will be an image to connect the other information to. It's kind of like having a Christmas tree and putting all kinds of different decorations on it.

Spelling Says A Lot About Hoo You Are.

(Yes, I spelled that wrong on purpose. It's sad how often I have to explain that.)

I think I have 'a sexy lid'...I mean I'm pretty sure I have dyslexia.

Spelling is one of my favourite things to memorize. This claim probably sounds exaggerated, like 'I love jogging', 'I love Grandma', or 'I love multivitamins', but I really do think spelling is awesome. My editor, whom I've never seen, asked me if I could write more on spelling and I was like '*#$&, yeah'. Sorry, I sneezed on the keyboard when I was trying to spell 'sure'. I love texts with proper grammar and spelling. I think it's awesome that *Cathy* has the name letters as *yacht*, that Jason Mraz has a last name that spells Mister A to Z or that *racecar* is spelled the same backwards. Ok, maybe I'm babbling a little because I'm actually recovering after my third brain surgery, so read on at your own risk. Right now I'm talking to my editor in my head, who looks a lot like the cartoon figure in the IKEA 'how-to' pamphlets. I should just leave this part out....

Helping someone with spelling can either be done over a few months of supervising methodical practice, or it is something that can be done informally

159

as you sit down with a child for a few minutes. Whether it is a child learning to read and write words for the first time, a student who struggles with basic language skills, or an adult learning English as a second language, using mnemonics to learn language can be an enjoyable and successful experience.

Three words that are often confused are *their*, *they're*, and *there*. Just like you can see the word 'ear' in 'hear', you can point out that the word 'there' has the word 'here' in it. These simple ways to focus are often enough, but they can be expanded. Imagining the 'i' in 'their' to be an ice cream cone that belongs to the soccer team will help a child remember that this word means 'belongs to them'. Gross.

Helping someone see letters as a picture will help them to see words as being more than just lines. It can be as easy as showing that there is an 'ant' on the 'plant' or the clouds 'owe you' some money (to remember the 'ou'). Since thinking of images works, one of the easiest ways to get better at spelling is to imagine an object inside of a word to remember the tricky part to spell. You don't have to memorize all the letters, just the ones that will give you trouble.

parallel

Imagine a set of railroad tracks going through the word. Since the a's and e's are in places that sound like those letters, the tricky part is where to put the two l's. Since the parallel tracks go through the middle of the word, this is where you put the two l's. You can even draw the tracks as you study this word.

Buddha

Of course you can imagine things however you wish, but I imagine the two d's in the name are like two marble columns of a monastery, the 'h' as a statue of Buddha, and the 'a' as a gong. If this offends you, then get your own floating, ancient, golden prince vision to remember the letters.

science

> Since this word is very tricky, especially for new spellers, you can imagine each letter in the word as an object on a science table: s: squiggly hose, c: clamp, i: bubbling beaker, e: copper wire, n: stand, then one more clamp and wire. When you write the word, make sure you can see each thing. And make sure they are in the right order, otherwise this is just art class and we might as well eat play dough. You won't have to do this for many words, but for this one it's fun.

cemetery

> Imagining a parking 'meter' in the middle of the graves will help you to remember there are only e's in this word, where many people would put an 'a' somewhere. And, yes, I know there is a 'y' at the end which is also a vowel. *Sometimes*. I wouldn't want to offend any of the 'y' people. It feels like they are always challenging me. Why? I don't know. They just are.

library

> Imagine a rare coin hidden in the middle of a library. This will help you to remember the three middle letters: 'rar'. The rest of the word should be fairly easy to remember. That is, of course, if you don't speak any English at all. I do wonder how you made it this far through the book, though.

Dessert in the Desert

> Dessert (like a sundae) and desert (a big sand lot) are often confused with each other. To help with this, imagine eating dessert with a silver spoon to remember 'ss' and a snake in the desert to remember one 's'.

'Oh' the Words

For words with o's and other vowels you can use round objects like eyes or oranges to create images. For *moon* you can think of a smiling moon with two eyes. For *cloud* you can imagine a cloud with one black eye, like the annoying one in *Trolls*. For *boat* you can imagine one full of o̲ranges and a̲pples.

Build words like you are using Lego blocks.

Larger words can be made from combining smaller words. To remember how to spell *attention* imagine setting up a scout post '**at** the **tent** with a **lion**'. Imagine a picture of **hot grap**es in a **h**ouse to remember the key letters in *photograph*. Imagine Big **Nate pass**ing a passion fruit to a **lion** to remember the letters in passionate.

You can focus on just one letter or all the letters that make up a word. Seeing letters and words as more than just lines and dots will not only help you with writing words, but with reading and understanding better too. It may or may not improve your karate moves.

The Alphabet

For my elementary students I came up with a picture for every letter of the alphabet as well as one for letters that usually go together.

Vowels

For vowels I use one image for soft sounds (that usually have two consonants after it) like ap̲ple, igloo, or umbrella and one for hard sounds like acorn, ice, or eagle. These images start with each letter and have the same shape. An apple is a soft fruit that is shaped like an 'a' but an acorn is a hard nut that is shaped like an 'a'.

Why? Because it's a letter too.

Some of the images helped my students understand certain rules. For the letter 'y' we used yarn needles. When you spell a word like 'happy', there is enough room at the end that they look like a 'y'. However if you add more letters, like in 'happiness', these needles get crowded together and look like just an 'i'. This helps you to remember to change a 'y' to an 'i' when you add an ending for words like beauty/beautiful, heavy/heaviness, or cry/cried.

Flowers in a Vase are always a good idea.

When you have one flower (which looks like an 'f'), it's beautiful, but it's just a flower. When you have more than one flower, you often put them in a vase. Using a flower for 'f' and a vase for 'v' helps kids remember how to spell words like wolves and knives. When there is one wolf (like one flower), then there is just an 'f' at the end. However, if there is more than one wolf, then it changes to a 'v' followed by 'es' (like more than one flower goes in a vase). This will help them remember to spell wives instead of 'wifes' or 'calves' instead of calfes.

duck puck buck

Often the letters that the self-diagnosed dyslexians mix up are letters 'b', 'p', 'd', and possibly 'q'. They claim they have trouble writing these on the right place on the line and facing the right direction. For the letter 'b', we use broomball. By first drawing a line down for the broom, followed by a circle for the ball, we fix both these problems. A broom cannot go through the ground, so it must rest on the line. Because it comes first, the line then the circle will get the 'b' facing in the right direction. It will take some work, probably more than twice, but it is a skill that can be mastered. The other letters work the same way. A dog's leash is drawn with the dog (circle) first and then the leash (line). Both of these must go on the line. The paper roll (like paper towels) has the paper first (the piece that dangles down) and the roll on the line. The quail tail has the round quail first and the tail hanging down below the line.

The Mighty 'C'

This is one of the coolest letters for spelling as it has so many connections. We use a 'crown' for the letter 'c' because it is shaped like one and has the right sound. For 'k' and 'q' (two letters that have the same sound), we use two people who wear crowns: a king and queen. To remember when a 'c' makes a soft sound (like an 's'), we think of a princess because the 'ce' and 'ss' - the letter sets that make an 's' sound - are right beside each other. The princess is also an 'icey' princess like Elsa (and yes, I know the word 'icey' is spelled incorrectly). These four letters remind us of the ways to make a soft 'c' sound which are 'ci' (city), 'cy', or 'ce'. We also think of a crown on a house or a 'church' for the 'ch' sound and the choir that sometimes sings, like how ch sometimes makes a hard 'c' sound. We make many of the same connections for the letter 'g', but I think that is enough for now.

Silence is golden

Once you have a picture for each letter, you can use these to remember the silent letters in some tricky words. Imagining the lamb silently using a broom, a king silently holding his 'K' shield by his knee, or a whale silently writing a letter home could be stories to remember the silent letters in *lamb*, *knee*, or *write*.

All the single letters, there's no reason why you can't find love too.

Other words like calendar often have one letter that trips us up. These letters may or may not be silent, depending on who is speaking... or paying attention. These words can include Arctic, pigeon, guitar, government, or raspberry.

The Alphabet (images)

	soft		hard
a	apple		acorn
e	egg		eagle
i	igloo		ice
o	octopus		orange
u	umbrella		ukulele

b	broom ball	d	dog leash
p	paper roll	q	quail tail

c	crown	k	king (shield)
		q	quail

	icey princess		
g	glass		

f	flower	v	vase

h	house	j	jazz (saxophone)
l	lamp	m	mountain
n	noodle	r	rabbit

s	snake	t	tack
w	whale	x	xylophone
y	yarn	z	zipper

You can use images for suffixes and prefixes to build larger words. I use these things to cover the root word of what I'm trying to remember. For example, a motorcycle helmet (my image for *protect*) covered in bees from a hive would be my image for protective. A life jacket with a dance costume sewn onto it would be my image for assistance.

able	(capable)	tablecloth
ant	(servant)	red ants
ance	(brilliance)	dance costume
city	(velocity)	skyscraper glass
ette	(kitchenette)	net
ic	(rhythmic)	ice
ive	(defective)	bees (from a hive)
ly	(closely)	lily
ness	(happiness)	Loch Ness scales
ish	(selfish)	fish scales
ous	(famous)	mouse fur
tion	(action)	hand lotion
dis	(disrespect)	dish soap bubbles
mis	(misread)	arrows (missed)
re	(redo)	pop cans (recycle)
un	(unlikely)	sunlight

Other times I combine two images such as a scary clown climbing a city skyscraper for scarcity. Some people use a separate image for each word and that works too. They might use a small science magnet for *attract*, a ballroom dancer for *attractive*, and a heavy duty magnet machine from a wrecking yard for *attraction*. No matter how you create images, as you practice, your collection of images will only get bigger and more detailed and your word skills will only get better.

What's in a Name?

*(You look familiar, but I can't remember your name.
I do know that you used to steal my lunch money.)*

**When a kid does something worth talking about at recess,
you'll remember that kid for life.**

Remembering names is one of the trickiest skills to master. At times we get a person's name mixed up with the name of their brother, sister, or cousin. Other times we get close but we say 'Kate' instead of 'Kathy' or 'David' instead of 'Darryl'. Sometimes we forget their name completely. We still try to carry on a conversation by saying things like "Hey, How are you doing? Is your family good? What are you doing now?" This buys some time while you go through the mental Rolodex of something that might make a name click.

Knowing a person's name has many upsides, but it's a skill only a few can master. Knowing a person's name can make a more personal connection that leads to more business. Socially, remembering a person's name makes you a more likeable person, which potentially leads to more close friendships. Remembering a person's name from history will allow you to recall more important facts about history. You get the idea. Remembering names is a powerful tool, like Excalibur to Arthur... except it's not a deadly, medieval weapon.

There are different ways to connect a name to a person. You can find a specific physical feature and connect an image of the person's name to it. For example, Blain has a birthmark shaped like an island on the back of his neck that you noticed right away. I know that the shape of an island is vague, but just go with it. To remember his name, imagine a 'plane' (which rhymes with 'Blain') landing on his island birthmark. The next time you see him and want to remember his name, look for a feature that you noticed the first time you met him. You see his birthmark, you'll remember the plane you imagined landing, and you'll remember that his name is Blain.

You can use this strategy with features like glasses, jewelry, clothing, tattoos, or facial features. To remember that Julia is the girl with the square, green glasses, image her glasses being decorated with sparkling 'jewels' (for 'Julia'). To remember that Noah is the kid you saw wearing the orange skateboarding shirt at the soccer game, imagine the skateboarder on his shirt doing extreme tricks on Noah's ark. To remember that Camilla is the girl with the heart tattoo, image a camel (for 'Camilla') eating a heart-shaped candy off of her arm where her tattoo is. When meeting a person again, you will have to think back to the first time you met and think about what feature stood out about them. This strategy works, but it will take some practice to master.

Another option is to think of what stands out in your mind when you think of a person. Maybe you remember them for being a good golfer, a regular at the library, the secretary at the school, or a stamp collector. It can be their job, hobby, sport, or just something you remember them doing. You can use these thoughts to connect an object for their name.

For example, to remember that the goalie of the soccer team is 'Brian', imagine him playing soccer and saving a brain (for 'Brian') from going into the net.

To remember that the captain of the fire department is Lucy, imagine she is eating a bowl of Lucky Charms (for 'Lucy') while her team is fighting a fire. To remember that the girl who always reads on the bench outside of the church is 'Sadie', imagine her sitting on a saddle (for 'Sadie') that bucks like a bronco beside the bench where she always reads. When using this strategy, you start by thinking of what pops up in your mind when you think of them, and then you can find the image for their name. This means that you have to be familiar with this person, spend some time getting to know them, or at least pretend you care about them. I know it's hard, but give it a try.

A technique I use involves making up a story about this person. Everyone has a story about a kid who did something in elementary school that no one can forget. For me it's when a kid in my eighth grade class forgot how to go down a hill on cross country skis and ended up gift-wrapping himself around a small evergreen tree. Some people end up on the news or a comedy show after mumbling phrases like, "Ok, hold my beer"; "I saw this on TV"; or "This might work". This could be the guy who opened his door while going through a car wash, the kid who tried petting the mother goose, or the girl in front of a hockey game crowd who thought she knew all the words to the national anthem. Every family has the stories they retell every holiday about someone getting tricked, hurt, or embarrassed. It's how they show their love. For me it was the time my sisters let me roll off the hood of the car when I was a baby because they were fighting over the 'good' bike. Stories are awesome.

When I need to remember someone's name, I start by creating a shocking, interesting, or funny story about them. It doesn't need to be true. In fact it is never true, so I can go crazy with it. I can imagine the person saving cats from a burning building, breaking the record for hiccups during an opera, face painting the president, back-flipping into a kiddie pool of whipped cream, attacking my garden gnome like a Jedi, falling into a mud puddle on the way to prom, or sneezing into Granny's birthday cake. I never have to tell anyone what's going on in my mind so no one will ever think I'm the weird kid in art class.

Because I don't have to rely on personal information about them, I don't have to get to know them. I never have to think about the painful home movies about their trip to Europe, listen to stories about how their cat did something cute on their kitchen table, or look on Facebook at their pictures of food they made for a night home alone. You also don't have to look for a unique physical feature like a birthmark or tattoo. People tend to get awkward when you spend time scanning their body.

These stories that you make will come back as soon as you recognize the person. Whenever I see my friend from volleyball, I instantly think of him riding a pink Hannah Montana bike. This will happen more as you use this strategy to remember names. And no, his name is not 'Hannah'. That would be a weird name for a guy. His name is 'Montana'.

Using stories to remember names is the same strategy you have used to remember all the information so far. You turn the name into an image and then include it with the story. If you haven't picked this up, the basis for memorization is making a story with things. Actually, I know you already understand this. I just had to reinforce it with dialogue.

To remember Olivia Pérez, I imagine that she is the captain of my little brother's lacrosse team. When she runs with her lacrosse stick, the crowd sprays her with olive oil from the top of the Eiffel Tower. Being the captain of the lacrosse team is something I'll remember the next time I see her because it agitates my brother. The olive oil will help me remember her first name: Olivia. The Eiffel Tower will help me remember her last name: Pérez (which sound like Paris).

To remember Logan Flores, I imagine that he is the one that stole my bike in grade two. When he took it, he rode it over a field of logs and flowers. I am always going to remember the guy who stole my favourite bike. The logs will help me remember his name is 'Logan' and the flowers will help me remember his last name is 'Flores'.

To remember Alex Young, I imagine she is the girl who knocked over the cake at my daughter's wedding. She falls because a young panda bear pushes her over an axel from a dump truck. The cake incident guarantees that I will always remember her face. The axel will help me remember her first name: 'Alex'. The young panda will help me remember her last name: 'Young'.

These stories will trigger emotions that in our mind's eye seem real. Psychologists believe that our mind cannot tell the difference between something that is real and something that is imagined. So when you create a story about someone you have just met, you have to create a memory of that person, similar to a father seeing his baby girl walk for the first time or a teenager getting his first kiss under the bleachers.

On the next page you will find some examples of images that you could use for names. When you create an image for a name, you only have to do it once. For example if you meet someone named 'Amber', you think of a crayon (because you read *Amber Brown is Not a Crayon*). The next time you meet someone named 'Amber', you can use this same image of a crayon again.

I have included just some examples of popular names from a list on Wikipedia. Don't feel bad if your name is not on the list. It's kind of like those racks at the gift store that have personalized key chains. There are always fifteen with 'Emma' but they are always sold out of your name. I feel your pain.

So to answer Shakespeare's question, "What's in a name?" our answer is imaginary objects, shocking stories, and traumatic memories.

Given Names:

Name	Association	Name	Association
Abigail	a big gull	Aiden	lifejacket (float aid)
Addison	adding machine	Andrew	Etch-a-sketch
Alexis	car axel	Anthony	ant on a 'thorny' rose
Allison	alley cat kitten	Benjamin	key on a kite string
Amelia	a meal	Brayden	branding iron
Anna	ant	Carter	horse and 'cart'
Aria	area rug	Christian	cross
Aubrey	brie cheese	Christopher	Christmas tree
Audrey	odd-shaped ray	Danny	Great Dane
Ava	Avatar	David	dove with a video
Avery	a furry bear	Dylan	rotary phone (dialing)
Brooklyn	brook	Ethan	ether
Camilla	camel	Gavin	cabin (rhymes)
Charlotte	spider	Henry	Oh Henry bar
Chloe	cloned sheep	Hunter	bow and arrow
Claire	clear bubble	Isaac	sack of glass eyes
Elizabeth	a lizard in a bath	Isaiah	hobbit (a slayer)
Ella	elephant	Jack	jack-in-the-box
Emily	family photo	James	jar of jam
Emma	M&M	Jaxon	jacks
Gabriella	gavel and brie	Jayden	jade
Grace	graceful swan	John	toilet
Hailey	hail chunks	Joseph	7 coffees (Joe seven)
Harper	harp	Joshua	Joshua tree
Isabella	bell with eyes	Julian	jewel
Leah	Lee jeans	Landon	London Bridge
Lillian	ant on a lily	Levi	lever
Madison	a mad son	Logan	log

Darren Mark Michalczuk

Mia	Mio	Lucas	Darth (Lucasfilm)
Natalie	gnat	Luke	Luke Skywalker
Olivia	olive oil	Mason	brick (mason)
Riley	rye bread	Matthew	gym mat
Sadie	saddle	Michael	microphone (Mike)
Samantha	sandwich (sammich)	Noah	Noah's Ark
Sarah	saran wrap	Ryan	rhino
Scarlett	Will Scarlet	Samuel	sad mule
Sophia	sofa	Sebastian	crab (Little Mermaid)
Victoria	trophy (victory)	William	apple (William Tell)

Surnames:

Adams	Addams family	Moore	suit
Allen	Allen wrench	Nichols	nickel
Baker	muffins	Palmer	palm tree
Barnes	barn	Parker	parking metre
Bennett	bonnet	Perez	pears
Black	licorice	Perry	fairy
Brown	brown crayon	Peterson	Peter Rabbit
Bryant	brain	Phillips	screwdriver
Burns	torch	Price	price gun
Campbell	soup can	Ramirez	ram with a rose
Carter	playing cards	Reed	library books
Clark	store clerk	Richardson	Richie Rich
Cole	coal	Rivera	riverboat
Coleman	Coleman stove	Roberts	robber
Cooper	copper wire	Robinson	Robin Hood
Cox	rooster	Rogers	CB radio
Crawford	crawfish	Ross	race flag

Edwards	Scissorhands	Sanders	sandman
Fisher	fisherman	Scott	paper towel
Flores	flowers	Shaw	satellite dish
Ford	Ford Mustang	Simpson	Homer
Graham	graham crackers	Smith	horseshoe
Grant	giant	Stewart	stewardess
Gray	statue	Sullivan	Sulley
Green	frog	Taylor	needle and thread
Hall	disco ball	Thomas	tank engine
Harris	Sasquatch (hairy)	Thompson	Tommy gun
Hawkins	hawk	Turner	record player
Jones	Jones pop bottle	Ward	prison warden
Kelly	killer whale	Warren	game warden
King	crown	Washington	washing machine
Knight	chess piece	Watson	Dr. Watson
Lewis	double bass (lows)	Webb	spider web
Long	snake	Wells	wishing well
Lopez	fruit 'loops'	West	cowboy hat
Marshall	marshmallow	White	snowman
Miller	windmill	Wright	feather pen
Mitchell	match	Young	baby

Darren Mark Michalczuk

MEMORY CHALLENGE

On the next page are some portrait pictures you can practice with. To start, you can remember each first name, and later, you can try memorizing each surname. Like the other challenges, you can time yourself to see how you do the first time. In life, you will have many opportunities to practice, but here is a good place to start using memory techniques.

For each person you can imagine what job or profession they have, focus on an article of clothing or physical feature, or create a story as to how you know each person. A person may look like a lumberjack, a tattoo artist, a tennis coach, or a snowboarder. You may want to focus on a pair of glasses, a hat, or a flannel shirt. Maybe a man looks like a used car salesman who sold you your first Camaro or a girl looks like your crush from third grade.

Once you have something that you'll remember the next time you see them, make a connection to an object that will help you remember the name. Maybe the lumberjack is picking up M&M's because her name is Emma. You can imagine rabbit ears on the guy who looks like an accountant because his name is the same as the rabbit from the children's story, Peter Cottontail. The girl who looks like a kindergarten teacher can have a wedding ring hanging from her glasses because her name is Mary.

Do what works for you, but if you need some help, there are suggestions on the following page. There are suggestions for first names and bolded words you can use for the surnames. There is no right or wrong way of doing things, as long as it works for you. You can test yourself on the following page.

NAMES

Cheat Sheet

- The lumberjack picks **M&M's** (Emma) from a tree under a full **moon**.
- The accountant wears **rabbit ears** (Peter) and pulls a **cart** full of eggs to work.
- The kindergarten teacher pops a **volleyball** with her wedding **ring** (Mary).
- The skater is cooking **horseshoes** on a **stove** (Steve).
- The tennis pro pours a jug of **shamrocks** (Patrick) into his **tomato soup**.
- The toothpaste model is a **janitor** (Jennifer) who sweeps up the **brown dirt**.
- The mad scientist is shooting **arrows** (Archer) at a **parking** metre.
- The yacht owner is feeding Froot **Loops** to a **mermaid** (Ariel).
- The yoga instructor is pouring **olive** (Olivia) oil over **Thomas** the Train.
- The tattoo artist has **keys** (Keith) to his safe full of **Chapman's** ice cream.
- The CEO keeps her hair back with **Charlotte**'s web and **copper** pins.
- The saxophone player plays on a **mason** jar wrapped with **Scotch** tape.
- The bank manager gets hit with **Caesar** salad and **Hershey** kisses.
- The dentist has a pet **martin** covered in **red paint** (Scarlet).
- The used car salesman uses his **walker** to carve out **Roman** numerals.
- The stewardess uses a **CB radio** to request a Hawaiian **lei** (Leah).
- The choir singer rings **bells** (Bella) for the **king** of the land.
- The accountant does **baking** for a blue **jay** (Jayden) in the back yard.
- The nurse rides a **saddled** horse (Sadie) over the **hill** to the hospital.
- The wilderness guide finds a **five dollar bill** (Benjamin) under an old **book**.

brain magic

Name Game

(I imagined Jermaine Jackson to remember a name, but later I couldn't remember if it was Michael, Tito, or Janet.)

Do you remember the kid from school who was kind of tall with dark hair and brown eyes?

When I think of my elementary school days, half the boys in my class were kind of tall and had dark hair and brown eyes. During these same years, most of my uncles were tall, wore a jacket that smelled like they had just come from an ABBA concert, and drove a red car from an 80s rock video. My teachers were mainly middle-aged females with long brown hair who wore dresses straight out of the Sears catalogue.

Now, I'm sure some of the names in this chapter are unfamiliar to you, but there was no way around it. To pick someone who was known and loved by all would be impossible. No matter what generation you are from, you have known about a celebrity who was popular and had a good reputation. Then, whether it was Donnie Osmond, Michael Jackson, or Justin Bieber, things fell apart. If you don't know who these people are, just look them up or just pretend you know them. The ideas are more important than the actual people.

If I were to use familiar people in a story in hopes of remembering their names, chances are I would mix them up. Personally, I wouldn't be able to tell if the image in my head was Mrs. Schmidt or Miss Daniels, Jeremy Julian or Danny Thompson, Uncle Mike or Uncle Trevor. I'd love for you to meet them, but I'm pretty sure at least two of them are in jail.

The same thing happens when I try to use names of objects to remember things. When seeing an image of a stereo in my mind, I can't remember if the name I was trying to remember sounded like 'Sony' or 'Samsung'. When seeing a car, I can't remember if the word I was trying to memorize rhymed with 'Ford' or 'Dodge'. I can't remember if the dog I imagined was named 'Spot', 'Rover', 'Buddy', 'Amadeus', or 'Davis Love the Third'. For these reasons, it is not ideal to use names for tools to remember information. However, there are some things you can do to make them work.

Using names can be tricky if the person or thing can be confused with something else. A young pop singer with blond hair and great dance moves could be one of several people. Trying to connect the brand name of a sweater might not be specific enough to lock in one name. Using a green highway sign to remember the name of a town has too many possibilities to count.

Using the name of something to remember information isn't a bad idea, but the person or object needs to be unique. The easiest way to do this is to add an object or an exaggerated feature. An image of Michael Jackson to remember the name 'Michael' over time may start to look like Tito or Jermaine or maybe even Janet. If the image of Michael is wearing his famous studded glove or red and black leather jacket, moonwalking across the floor, or walking a black panther, then it will be unmistakable. If you don't know who any of the Jacksons are, just Google 'The Jackson 5', 'Thriller', or 'wardrobe malfunction'.

To make objects with names easier to remember, you can make certain features stand out by magnifying them, so to speak. Using Kobe Bryant to remember a name will work better if you focus on when he was younger and had his signature hair and yellow 'Lakers' jersey. You can also exaggerate these features, such as making his hair higher than usual and the logo on his shirt bigger. Think of the street artists who draw caricatures of people by exaggerating unique features.

You could also give a person or thing a unique object to define it. If you imagine Sylvester Stallone (assuming you know who he is), thinking of a muscular action star with a deep voice probably won't be enough. There are too many of those already like Vin Diesel, Arnold Schwarzenegger, or Bruce Willis. If you have seen some of Sylvester Stallone's movies you could imagine him with long hair, a black headband, and a survival knife from *Rambo*; or a pair of boxing gloves from *Rocky*; or even a beret, sunglasses, and black vest from *The Expendables*.

If you are using Olivia Newton John, you could imagine her with a white headband from her "Physical" video and the leather jacket and perm from *Grease*. For Benjamin Franklin you could imagine him flying his famous kite and key. Dominic Toretto could be holding a wrench standing next to his Dodge Charger. Otherwise you might mix these people up with Farrah Fawcett, George Washington, and Jason Statham respectively. And yes, I know that Dom is only a fictional character, but it doesn't matter in the world of your memory.

When choosing people for names, remember that there is often more than one possibility. If you need someone for the name 'John', you could use John Cena with his wrestling championship belt, John Travolta with his dress from *Hairspray*, or John Lennon with his famous glasses and piano. If you need someone for 'Jennifer', you could think of Jennifer Aniston with her umbrella from the opening credits of *Friends*, Jennifer Lopez with her blocks (since she is Jenny from the block), or Jennifer Lawrence with her bow and fire dress from

The Hunger Games. It is your mind and your memory palace, so you let in whomever you want. Just remember that if you let in the wrong two people at the same time, you're going to have trouble. The people in my head often fight, like really bad, so now I've got no one to talk to.

Celebrity Images:

Sydney Crosby	penguin	Beyoncé	halo
Tom Hanks	astronaut	Chris Hemsworth	hammer
Jack Nicholson	ax	Mark Hamill	light saber
Keanu Reeves	overcoat	Leo DiCaprio	lion
Brad Pitt	bar of soap	Marlon Brando	marionette
Bill Murray	bear	Tim McGraw	outlaw
Justin Bieber	beaver	Zac Efron	paper moon
Garth Brooks	belt buckle	Nadia Comaneci	parallel bars
Justin Timberlake	Bobo	Adele	phone booth
Michael Jordan	bull	Johnny Depp	pirate hat
Harrison Ford	bull whip	Elvis Presley	sandwich
Michael Phelps	butterfly	Chris Evans	shield
Tim Allen	Buzz	Scarlett Johansson	snake
Babe Ruth	chocolate bar	Madonna	suspenders
Michael J. Fox	DeLorean	Jim Carrey	The Grinch
Taylor Swift	felt marker	Tiger Woods	tiger
Tom Cruise	fighter jet	Emma Watson	wand
Russell Crowe	gladiator	John Lennon	white piano
Elijah Wood	gold ring	Miley Cyrus	wrecking ball
Jason Mraz	guitar	Michael Jackson	zombie

zookeeper

MEMORY CHALLENGE

For this challenge you will memorize the names of animals that you might find at the City Zoo. There are many things besides people that can have names. Some people have a special name for their car. Boats are often given female names or names that are a play on words. Some weirdoes even name their golf clubs. Anything in the world can be given a name. Though we can't practice everything at once, we can start with wild animals.

This is an exercise I do with my students as a way to practice memory skills. I tell them to imagine being a zookeeper and part of the job is to memorize the names of each animal, first and last. Knowing their names helps keep a good relationship with them. You don't want to have an alligator in a bad mood. Knowing their names will also help to get the food and medicine to the right animal. Prozac will do nothing for a hippo with a urinary tract infection and antibiotics won't help a turtle suffering from depression.

When my students see each animal, I encourage them to imagine that each animal has a cool personality trait or special skill. Maybe the hippo is a great lounge singer. The iguana could be a grumpy old man who constantly complains about the temperature of the room. The fox could be a convicted bank robber who escaped from prison earlier this morning. These stories make it a little easier to remember the animals and the story to remember their name(s).

When you create stories to remember each name, be sure to have an object. Something you can see or touch will be easier to remember than a string of letters. A good rule of thumb (or finger or leg or spleen or whatever you use to make rules) is that what you use to memorize the name should be something you are able to hold in your hands.

zookeeper

Cheat Sheet

- A **zebra** smashes **Sara** Lee pudding with an ampersand (**Anderson**) stamp.
- A **gator** is enjoying **fluffy** cotton candy wrapped around a copper pipe (**Copper**).
- A **fox** uses a **Lucas**film lightsaber to hit a **Wilson** volleyball over the net.
- A **hippo** uses a shovel to get more (**Moore**) jewels (**Julie**) from a pile.
- A **water buffalo** drives JFK's car (**Kennedy**) through a **Shaw** satellite.
- An **elephant** swings a **bell** (Belle) to deflect bullets from a zealous hunter (**Gonzalez**).
- A **pelican** is stuffing Wednesday **Adams** into **Oscar**'s trash can.
- A **warthog** is using **Jasmine** flowers to decorate the mayor's (**Myers**) hat.
- An **iguana** cooks on a stove (**Steve**) balanced on a cloud-shaped stone (**Gladstone**).
- A **turkey** is covering a crawfish (**Crawford**) with ChapStick (**Chapman**).
- A **leopard** is throwing M&M's (**Emma**) at a hospital patient's cast (**Castro**).
- A **komodo dragon** is making a boom (**Boomer**) in a boxing ring with a chess **bishop**.
- A **chipmunk** is making a house for a chicken (**Fowler**) with **driftwood**.
- A **deer** is playing tennis on a court (**Courtney**) covered with straws (**Estrada**).
- A **turtle** crawls across **Charlotte**'s web wearing a maid's uniform (**Chambers**).
- A **beaver** smashes her phone with OMG (**Imogen**) on a **steel** beam.
- A **badger** uses a wide-mouthed **mason** jar to catch a fish (**Fischer**).
- A **wolf** destroys **Amadeus**'s piano with a World War II canon (**Canon**).
- A **meerkat** stores **pebbles** in a **Maxwell** House coffee can.
- A **rhino** plays the har**monica** while sitting in an outhouse (**Schmidt**).

there will be blank pages.

(Donner, Dancer, Blitzen, Comet, Vixen, Cupid, Prancer, ...I think I missed one...)

Even when you learn to memorize one hundred things, you may miss one or two.

When you start memorizing information, you may notice that you miss some things. For example, if you memorize a list of 20 items, at first you may only remember 17 or 18. As you practice memorizing, these missing pieces will help you fine-tune your memory skills. Think of taking a look at these 'blanks' as a way of troubleshooting your memory.

Things

When first memorizing a list of words, many people miss the ones that are *adjectives*, mainly because they don't turn these words into objects. For example if the eighth word on a list of 20 words is 'beautiful', then this word is something you can see or touch. When using the eighth memory hook (spider), some people will think of a very *beautiful* spider: the seductive eyes, the relaxed pose, and the ever so subtle vibe the spider is sending out in the world. This image will be something you really have to pay attention to in order to remember it. Ask any guy that has tried to read the subtle body language of a woman to find out what she is thinking. Subtle is tough.

Having two separate objects, one for the number '8' (spider) and one for the word beautiful (dress), is much more obvious and easier to remember. A better image might be a spider wearing a beautiful dress. This would give the mind more to retrieve the next time it goes looking for this memory. The vibrant colours, the intricate floral designs, and the flowing folds stand out in the mind, not to mention the sparkly earrings, high-maintenance-girl hat, and high heel shoes. Instead of giving an object a quality, create another object for each piece of information and you will be able to remember more.

Action

People sometimes miss information when things are stationary. For example, if the third word on a list is 'iguana', then you might create an image of an iguana sitting on a tricycle. If nothing in this image moves, then things may blend together. When the memory is revisited, the iguana could look like moss, a tree branch, or even a green blanket. Think of a hunter in camouflage standing in front of a background of trees. If he doesn't move, then he blends. If he moves, however, then it becomes very easy to see him, especially if his moves are big, unique, and interesting.

If we are to remember an iguana on a tricycle, have him ride the tricycle as if he were Tony Hawk at a skateboard park, crash the tricycle as if he were in the 'Running of the Bulls', or dance like a ballerina during a performance of 'Swan Lake'. With these movements it will be easier to see the long tail, the row of spines running down its back, the texture of its skin, and the unique body movements of an iguana. Movement adds another dimension to memories and brings them to life.

Uniqueness

As you create images in your mind, for many words you will only have to do this once. For example, if you use a flower for the word 'beautiful', then you will only have to do this once, especially if you use a very specific and unique flower. The next time you come across the word beautiful, you will already have an image. A blue tiger lily with exactly four petals is something that doesn't exist in nature, making it very unlikely this image will be needed for another word. If you choose to use a flower for something else, such as for 'fragility' or 'aroma', you simply use another flower with distinctly different features.

This means that you can exaggerate the features as well. If you need to create an object in your mind for the word 'monitor', you could imagine a heart monitor for a hospital. Even better than this, you could use a computer monitor, choosing an awesome, latest edition model. Using a green-screen monitor from the 80s is not going to be as effective as the next-year model with a realistic video feed of a hummingbird on it, like you would see for sale in an electronics store.

For the word 'automatic', a 2017 red Lamborghini will work much better than a 1971 wood-panel station wagon, unless of course you are an accountant with a fondness for pine. A champagne glass with gold trim may work better than an ordinary tumbler. An ancient arrowhead may work better than a plain, round rock. You get the idea.

For the word 'appreciate', the first image might be a thank-you card, but this could easily be confused for a postcard from Grandma's trip to the local orchard or a coupon for 10% off an oil change. A better object might be a large bouquet of flowers. The bigger and more colourful the flowers, the more they will stick in the mind. Choose objects that are unique and 'awesome'. You can choose anything in the world, no matter how expensive, rare, or extravagant it is. After all, you are not paying for these memories. They are one hundred percent free, so go crazy.

Dead Air

As you practice your memory skills, you will be able to find better ways to create objects and stories in your mind. When you recall information and find a memory, then you should recreate the image. I know that sounds like you should be on a beach on some tropical island to relax, but trust me: 'recreate' has another meaning. I am a qualified fourth grade teacher. (If you don't believe me, I'll have to show you how I can make six different words from the letters on a stop sign.)

Make the image again. Be sure you have a distinct object for each piece of information. Make the objects move and interact together. Use objects that are unique and easy to remember. This will help you to remember more.

If you are still looking for more ways to improve your mind, don't worry. There is still more book to read. Now that I think about it, being on a beach on a tropical island couldn't hurt. You do remember more when you are relaxed. Go ahead and check your bank account and I'll wait here.

Hunting Ghosts

Sometimes you will look for information in your memory palace and you will find an image that you have created before for a different list. These 'ghost' images aren't usually a big problem, and they are easy to fix. Usually you will know the difference between an image you created a while ago and one that is fresh in your mind. However, you can go through the memory palace you are about to use. Imagining each memory hook being empty will 'clear' it so that it is ready to hold new information. It will help you see it more clearly and give you one more practice with it. It's like your coach making you do one more lap, except you don't have to worry about making the team, weight issues, personal hygiene, or acne from going through puberty way too early.

As you practice, you will find what works and what doesn't. Paying attention to the images that you remember and the ones that you don't will help you learn about your own personal learning style.

Map Maker

MEMORY CHALLENGE

Reading maps is a difficult task, and trying to remember not only the names but the shapes and locations on a page can be nearly impossible for some people. This challenge is going to be difficult, really difficult. Here you can practice seeing the lines that make up a country, province, or state as an object and create a story to remember the names connected with it.

Most people see the country of Italy as the shape of a boot. Most other countries or provinces don't look like anything (except Saskatchewan, which looks like a skyscraper), so you'll have to use your imagination.

Think of what the shape of the lines reminds you of, even if it doesn't fit perfectly. Once you have something in mind, you can use this object to remember the name of the country. You can also use parts of this object to remember locations such as the capital city, rivers, landmarks, or geographical features. For example, on the country that looks like a goldfish, you could imagine mountains above its eye, a river going across its tail, or a university building on the edge of its dorsal fin. For now, however, we'll just worry about the capital cities. You can try the other stuff on your own. You do have a life outside of this book.

The 'states' on the next page show some straight edges like one with borders, jagged edges like those with a coast, and irregular edges like those with natural borders. For the names, I just reached into a Scrabble bag.

| Matchee | Engia | Obajo |
| Dorsvil | Eleflui | Cowro |

| Occra | Berde | Carakes |
| Glavra | Suisland | Varseau |

| Dhaki | Freeton | Trelski |
| Cyrea | Myrlan | Rakistam |

| Laoss | Crissau | Feiro |
| Prian | Armia | Dreigai |

Map Maker

Cheat Sheet

Imagine:

- A feather floats over a village of doors (Dorsvil). Hold a burning match where the feather part starts to remember Matchee is the capital.
- An **ele**phant with the **flu** (Eleflui) sneezes out a **dragonfly** which was cleaning its eye with **England**'s flag (Engia).
- A **crow** (Cowro) tries to steal a woman's shoe. She puts her heel down and crushes a tiny **orange banjo** (Obajo).
- Use a glove (Glava) to play catch with a clam. An **orca** (Occra) sits in the middle of the clam like she is queen of the ocean.
- A **bird** (Berde) lifts a goldfish out of an aquarium. On its eye is the tiny **land** made of **Swiss** cheese (Suisland).
- An alien has a baby duck called **Ducky** (Dhaki) who puts Froot Loops **cereal** (cyria) in his navel. Animals are so weird...
- **Merlin** (Myrlan) finds an arrowhead for his spell. Through the hole you use for a necklace flies a **free** bird that weighs a **ton** (Freeton).
- An **ele**phant with the **flu** (Eleflui) sneezes out a **dragonfly**. A beautiful woman puts her heel down on an **orange banjo** (Obajo).

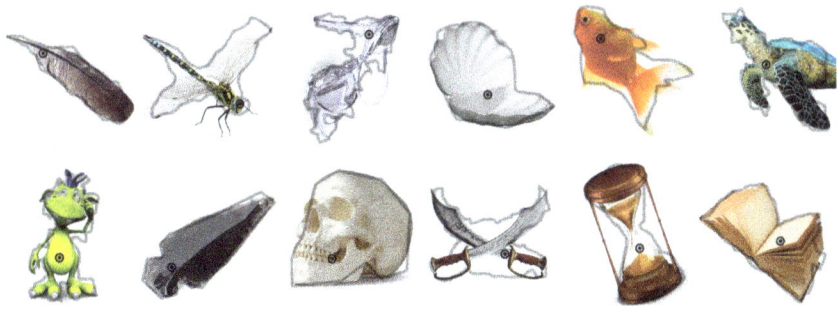

Imagine me, like one of your french words.

---

*(Even though I don't understand the words,
I still know what to do at a red octagon.)*

What do a glass of water, a bass, and a flower have in common? Probably nothing. I'm just checking to see if anyone reads these bolded sentences.

Actually they do have something in common. They are all part of my story to remember the French word for water. I think of playing a bass to make a beautiful flower grow in a glass of water. As I imagine the vibrating water and the silky orange petals, I think of the 'low' sounds of the bass (which sound like the French word 'l'eau'). I also think of how this word is spelled with the same letters you'd find in beautiful.

Some French words are easy to remember. The French word for 'orange' is 'orange'. I guess this makes sense, but not all translations are this easy. Here are some images that will show some ways to remember French vocabulary.

Learning to remember the meanings of words is something that can be done with the skills you have already learned. Simply turn the French word into an object, then turn its definition into an object, and connect them both using a story. It is like putting things in a memory palace, with the shelf being the image of the definition. When you think of the definition, or the English word you want to translate, you will remember the object for the French word.

tree: arbre

Imagine a barber playing hide and seek in a big oak tree. The letters in 'barber' are similar to the letters in 'arbre', which is the French word for 'tree'.

sea: mer

Imagine a 'meerkat' swimming in the Arctic 'sea' with a pair of butterfly water-wings. The first letters of 'meerkat' are similar to 'mer', which is the French word for 'sea'.

garden: cour

Imagine a couple of rabbits playing tennis on a tennis court in the middle of your garden. The first letters in 'court' are the same as 'cour', which is the French word for 'garden'.

bear: ours

Imagine a bear speed-stacking for hours, using an hourglass for a timer. The word 'hours' has the same letters as 'ours', which is the French word for 'bear'.

horse: cheval

Imagine a horse using a shovel to dig a tunnel. The word 'shovel' rhymes with 'cheval', which is the French word for 'horse'.

sink: lavabo

Imagine a titanium microphone (used by Demi Lovato) talking to you from under the bubbles in a sink. The word 'lavabo' sounds like 'Lovato', a singer famous for the song "Titanium", and is the French word for sink.

strawberry: fraise

Imagine a freezer overflowing with strawberries. The word 'freeze' sounds the same as 'fraise', which is the French word for strawberry.

You want to create images or stories that trigger the memory for the word. Sometimes all you need is a few letters to remember how a word is spelled. Focus on the smaller words, sounds, or odd letters and this will help you to spell the words correctly.

As with all images, images that have details, trigger the senses, or are out-of-the-ordinary will be easier to remember. As you practice, it will get easier and easier.

Here are more French words to practice with some images to use:

shower	douche	(Old Dutch chips)
brakes	freins	(Friends cast with umbrellas)
car jack	cric	(Jiminy Cricket)
tank	char	(charcoal)
winter	hiver	(hoover)
drums	tambours	(tame boars)
stove	poêle	(north pole)
saw	scie	(science beaker)
staple	agrafe	(a giraffe)
lemon	citron	(city runner)

Some languages are not letter-based, but symbol-based, such as Chinese. Here are some English words translated into traditional Chinese. As each symbol is specific, the details of your story should reflect how to write each character.

fire: 火

Imagine a wishbone running away from a forest fire carrying a golf tee and a small bag of gold.

cow: 牛

Imagine a cow working out on the beams of a pirate ship while a parrot yells fitness tips at her.

water: 水

Imagine pouring water over a slide while a parrot slides down it and an injured number seven leans on the ladder.

hundred: 百

Imagine a skeleton (100 object) going for a ride in a shopping cart (view from the rear) with a racing fin on the back.

As mentioned at the beginning of this book, it would be great to have benchmarks to use as comparisons. For learning, few people can remember as quickly as people who use these memorization methods. If you consider the people who rank in competitions such as the 'World Memory Competitions', it is easy to see what amazing feats these people are capable of, but also how many of them use these types of memorization strategies. If you want an exact percentage of how many, it's about... all of them.

It is also interesting to see the correlation between countries where these memory athletes are from and how successful these countries are academically. It only makes sense though. If you can memorize hundreds of vocabulary words, content and page numbers, important dates, key words, and names of important people, then learning in general will become much easier.

Learn to take Notes.

*(Anyone can learn music;
you just have to look at it the right way.)*

**Saying 'Every Good Boy Deserves Fudge' is ok,
but it's still like counting on your fingers to add.**

There is a belief that only certain people can learn music. When you ask some people if they play music, they often hide behind the humour of insecure comments like "I can play the radio." They believe that you must start learning music soon after learning to walk in order to master instruments like the piano or violin.

I remember a field trip where the kids had a chance to see creatures of all varieties, including reptiles and amphibians. Part of the tour was giving each child a chance to hold a snake. This was obviously the most exciting part and for some, a memory that would last a lifetime. The ranger told me that many people develop a fear of snakes because of the unknown. A snake has a unique and unfamiliar way of moving that can only be understood by holding an actual snake. He said that if children have a chance to experience this, the chances of developing a fear of snakes is essentially zero.

I guess the same can be said for music. I have taught music for many years and found that all students can learn to play an instrument. In one school I taught all of the music classes from grades four to six. The students learned to play keyboard instruments (electronic pianos and xylophones), guitars, violins, and of course the symbolic instrument of traditional elementary school music: the recorder. I can honestly say that all of them learned to play well, including melodies, harmonies, and chords.

One Christmas I was excited when several groups were able to play four-part harmonies of songs like "The First Noel" and "We Three Kings". Each child played a different set of notes, but when they played together it created a stereo-like sound that you would expect to hear in a church service or a high school concert. Out of roughly 50 students, all of them learned to play an instrument; and by the end of the year, many could play two or three. Many of the parents also bought instruments for their children to practice with at home, which was impressive considering it was a mainly farming community.

Learning music is understandably a daunting task. Written music is a set of abstract symbols that is a cross between math and language. Notes are written in an alphabet that only goes up to the letter 'g', but it has no letters. Instead of having a symbol to mark each note, each note is represented by an oval shape that is sometimes filled in or drawn with a vertical line attached. Finding and knowing the line or shape it rests on is the only way to know which note it is. The shape of the dot shows how long each note is played for. A hollow oval is played for four times as long as a solid oval with a line. I get it. It's hard.

The best way to learn music, however, is to start with the same method we use to learn names and numbers. By turning each note into an image and then connecting this image to a place, you can learn to read the notes on sheet music and then find these notes on an instrument.

Though this method will work with any instrument such as a clarinet, piano, or guitar, we'll start with a recorder. A recorder is an inexpensive instrument that you'll find in most elementary schools. It often comes with a guide to show how each note is played. Though many people cringe at the thought of listening to a seven-year-old play "Hot Cross Buns", when it is played well, especially with harmonies, it can be a very entertaining instrument.

A Note

Notes are written on a staff, or a set of five lines. If we imagine the middle line being a branch of a tree, we can learn the first note. Imagine an apple hanging off the middle line (the branch). Now hold your recorder, which you obviously keep in your back pocket, as if you were holding an apple with your index and middle finger covering the top two holes and your thumb covering the bottom hole. When you see the note hanging off the middle line, you will know how to hold the recorder to play an 'A' note.

E Note

Imagine the top two lines of the staff being power lines that you might see along a highway. Imagine the note between these lines being an eagle flying. Imagine the thinnest string of your violin, which you obviously have in your closet, being made of eagle feathers. When you see the note between the top two lines, you will remember that this note is an 'e' and you will know which string to play on a violin.

brain magic

B Note

You can imagine a butterfly flying through the middle of the staff to remember that the note on the middle line is a 'b' (for butterfly). On a guitar, imagine a butterfly landing on the second string from the bottom. When you see the note in the middle of the staff, you will know to pluck the second string from the bottom on your guitar.

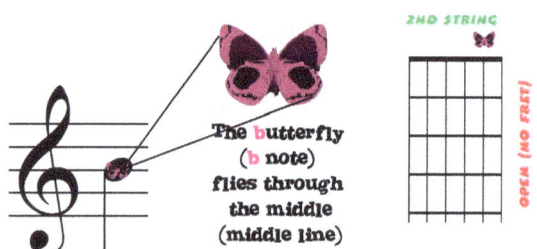

D Note

You can imagine a dog nose sniffing just under the table to remember that the note just below the bottom line is a 'd' (for dog). To find this note on a piano, imagine the set of two black keys being a dog house and the key inside being the dog. When you see the note under the bottom line of the staff, you know to play the key in between the two black keys.

Using this method takes away the finger-counting style of learning notes with the traditional mnemonic 'Every Good Boy Deserves Fudge'. You can look at

Darren Mark Michalczuk

a line or space and instantly see the image that represents the note without counting. After some practice, you can look at a note and instantly know how to play it on an instrument. Reading notes to play melodies happens much faster when you don't have to count the lines or spaces.

Reading notes is key to learning to play an instrument. Learning to read notes quickly and easily with music is comparative to being able to sight-read words without sounding out letters when reading a book or multiplying numbers without counting fingers or sets when solving math problems. It allows a new musician to focus on things other than the basics.

Reading tempo, chords, harmonies, or key signatures are things that can be learned once reading notes becomes easy. These skills can also be learned using the same skills.

We use the 'rock and roll horns' (which is basically the first, fourth, and fifth fingers) to remember the common chord pattern (I, IV, and V) for campfire songs. Most campfire songs are played with chords G(I), C(4), and D(5).

You can remember the notes in chords by assigning a name to each image. A chord is a set of notes that sound good together. For example, an 'A' (minor) chord is a made up of 'a' notes, 'c' notes, and 'e' notes. When you play these notes together, they sound good. To remember the notes in this chord, imagine that the apple (the image for 'a' note) is an 'ACE' brand apple to help you remember the three notes in the A minor chord.

Music is a passion of mine. I have had many experiences that I wish I could fully describe. Using memory skills to master notes and other skills is just the start. Once children (and willing adults) get skilled with notes, then the real magic happens.

After two months of violin practice, two girls played a lullaby I wrote for Wilbur during a grade two production of *Charlotte's Web*. They crouched behind a bale and played the song by heart. I remember years later going to a high school concert where two grade twelve girls played a similar song. All I could think was if someone closed their eyes and listened to these two songs, they wouldn't be able to tell who was playing violin: grade two students or seniors from high school.

I wrote two extra verses to the "Cups" song by Anna Kendrick. *Pitch Perfect* was a popular movie and the girls in my class learned to do the percussion sequence from YouTube videos as an accompaniment. They sang the song on field trips, at recess, and I was even able to fit it into one of our plays.

(third verse)

I got my ticket for the long way 'round.
The one I hope I'll take with you.
We'll make friends along the way.
We'll sing songs that last for days.
We'll make sweet memories is that okay.

When I'm gone
When I'm gone

You're gonna miss me when I'm gone.
You're gonna miss me now and then.
You're gonna miss me my best friend.
Oh, I know you're gonna miss me when I'm gone.

(fourth verse)

I got my ticket for the long way home.
With fields of green and skies of blue.
Close your eyes, I'll count the cars.
We'll ride 'til we see the stars.
Long talks with someone else just wouldn't do.

When I'm gone. When I'm gone.
You're gonna miss me when I'm gone.

You're gonna miss me if you stay.
You're gonna miss me every day.
Oh you're gonna miss me when I'm gone.

One night at home, my son figured out the melody to "Abraham's Daughter" on recorder and taught it to his little sister. No, I didn't let them watch *The Hunger Games*. While she practiced the steady string of notes, he figured out the chords. They played it together a day later in front of a group of long-term care residents. An attentive older brother played to keep time with his sister while she stretched her tiny fingers to cover the holes of the recorder. It was impromptu and beautiful.

Each year I have my homeroom class put on a drama production that I write. We have done *Hood* (our version of *Robin Hood*), *Oz* (my version of *The*

Wizard of Oz), and *Alice* (my version of *Alice in Wonderland*). After I realized I hadn't communicated things well enough and my five-year-old daughter was expecting to sing during my class's production of *Hood*, I knelt down to explain to her that the play was over and what a horrible father I was.

Before I could say anything an amazing parent gathered the audience so she could sing "The Show" from *Moneyball* to close out the show. I plucked the chords on guitar as she started off with "I'm just a little girl caught in the middle..." while parents stood and listened on the stage of our Cultural Arts Theatre. She rocked it.

I wish I could share these experiences with more than just words on paper. It's not simply a special moment or a perfectly timed snapshot, but the result of releasing the genius that exists inside all of us. These experiences don't happen by accident.

They happen when people see things differently.

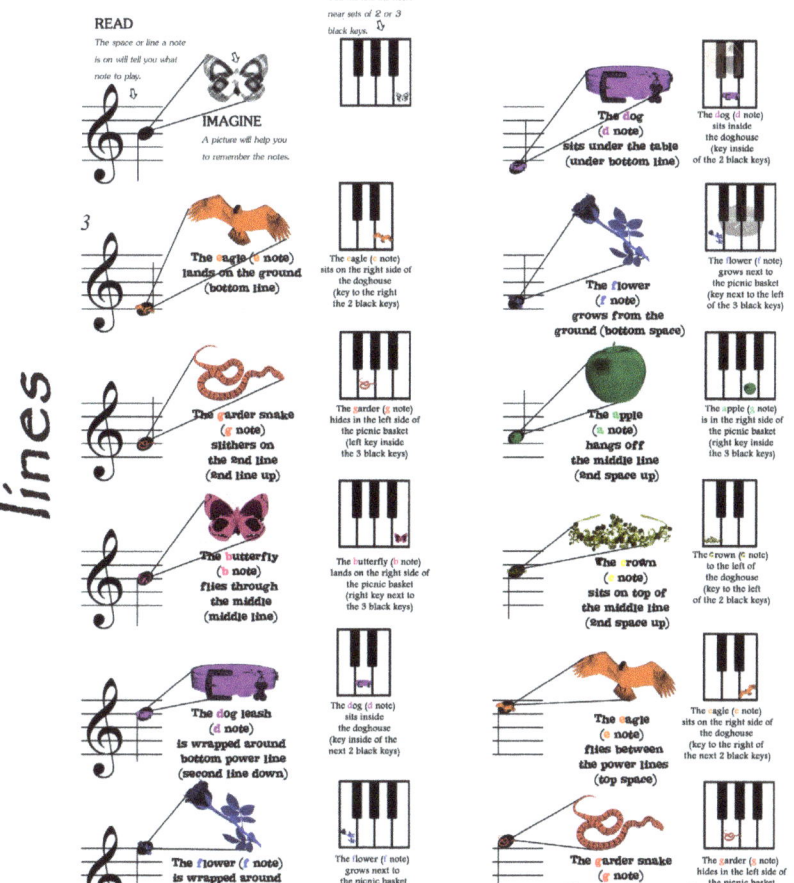

Darren Mark Michalczuk

i've hidden one more memory secret.

---

*(Like the FedEx logo,
there are some things you can't unsee.)*

**A butterfly chained to a mountain is not only cool to look at,
it's a metaphor for everything you've learned so far.**

If you have ever paid close attention to the 'FedEx' logo, then you may have noticed something interesting about it. The person who designed it, Lindon Leader, became very wealthy and famous for his creation. Aside from being simple, bold, and colourful, it has a secret design hidden in it. By using a specific font he was able to create a hidden image with the negative space between the letters 'E' and 'x'. I can't show it here as I'm sure I'd be breaking some copyright infringement, so you will have to look for it the next time you see or Google this logo. Now that I've written it, I'll have to check to see if it's okay to use the word 'Google'.

When you do see it, every time you see the FedEx logo, it's tough not to see it. It is a white arrow that points to the right near the end of the logo. It's a symbol for progress, it points in the right direction, and it's a hidden secret just like the prize at the bottom of a box of cereal. It doesn't get any more awesome than that.

Now I know I'll never be able to match this, but I did create a logo for this memory book that I'm very happy with. If you look at the bottom right-hand corner of the front of this book, you will see our logo. It is the name 'BRAINMAGIC.CA'. There are three hidden images in this logo that represent the basis for memorization in its simplest form. I show this to people who learn the system as a simple 'cheat sheet' note to refer back to.

The first symbol in the logo is the first letter 'A' drawn as a mountain. This was carefully chosen to represent a solid foundation to put information. An example of this could be one of the objects in our 'memory palaces': an image that is always going to be there to store information. For example, a spider, the eighth hook in the 'Kids Palace' memory palace, is something we use to store information. It will always be the eighth place in our mind, and an anchor to act as a hook to hang something we want to remember. This could also be a story about a person who we will never forget. This story is a solid place in our mind that we can always go back to and find. It could also be an image of a giant tooth that you use for the dentist's office. This is something that will always be in the mind to hold information such as a phone number. These anchors or rocks are solid places that never move or change so that you can find them easily, much like a mountain.

The second symbol is the chain that connects the letter 'A' to the 'B' (just like in the expression 'point A to point B'). This chain represents all the ways we connect images. Essentially, this chain is in the form of a story. These stories which 'chain' or 'glue' information to places in our mind must be memorable. They should include our senses like the sight, sound, or smell of objects. They should be out-of-the-ordinary, trigger emotions, or be larger than life. They should be personal or unique to each person. These stories will ensure that the information in these stories will stay connected to places in your mind.

These images show all the ways to make the stories you create be more memorable. As you practice storing information using images and stories, you will become better and faster. You will be able to visualize the pattern of a lumberjack shirt, the smell of chlorine from a swimming pool, or the sound of a St. Bernard. You will clearly see a rhino driving a taxi, a raven writing on a chalkboard, or a willow tree doing the Macarena. Imagining a snow globe lighting up like a disco ball, a remote control transforming into an '84 Trans Am, or a street sign folding into an origami swan is something you will be able to do at will.

At first you may create stories with elaborate details, complex emotions, and sound logic. Maybe to remember a word on a list you'll think of a snail finding a gold pendant - a clue left by his father that leads to pirate treasure. As you become better at creating memories, you may only need a short story with a single, simple action. Maybe to remember a science term you will imagine a grizzly bear diving into a pool.

With time and practice you will be able to create clear, memorable, stories more quickly and with less effort. You'll be amazed at how much you will be able to remember, especially if you think of what you were able to do before you learned these skills. Stories with these elements will help you connect information to places where you can find them in your mind, much like a chain.

The third symbol is the butterfly. This represents how you change information into things, the same way that a simple, boring caterpillar changes to a colourful, vibrant butterfly. A butterfly could be an image for the word 'beautiful', 'change', or 'delicate'. A volleyball could be an image for the name 'Wilson'. A spider could be an image for the number '8'. The mind sees images much easier than letters, numbers, or symbols.

These images can be anything that works for you. To remember the word 'anger', maybe you will think of a boiling kettle. Someone else may think of 'Anger', the red character shaped like a brick from Pixar's *Inside Out*. Others may think of the Hulk.

With practice you will be able to change any piece of information into an image. A bathtub is an image that will come to mind when you think of the name 'Beth'. The famous opera house shaped like sails will come to mind when you read the name 'Sydney'. When you see the number '3' you'll automatically see a tricycle. Information in the form of letters, numbers, symbols, or abstract ideas will become concrete objects in the mind that are easy to see and find.

The image of the butterfly chained to a mountain shows how to remember things easily. It shows the three basic steps to remembering things. By changing information into an image (butterfly) and creating a story (chain) to connect it to a place we can find (mountain), we can remember almost anything.

With these three steps, your memories will become interesting and engaging. Dry information like historical dates, phone numbers, or class notes will become things you will want to revisit in places in your mind that you can easily find. Much like sports highlights, action movies, or Super Bowl commercials, your mind will become a TV screen of great channels to remember anything from science terms for a biology test, to items on a grocery list, to license plate numbers.

This was a poster I used in 2000.

This is the poster I used in 2017.

Darren Mark Michalczuk

the twelfth poster

*(Eleven is just not an easy number to work with.
Try making even soccer teams from a group of eleven.)*

**Time to review what you've learned so far,
like this book isn't repetitive enough already.**

When I made the memory palaces into posters, I had exactly eleven (not including the body list). I made one more poster to make it an even dozen that was easier to put on the wall without having an OCD breakdown. For the last poster I chose ten strategies that helped me remember key strategies, like a 'cheat sheet' of memory tools.

Lemon   *Senses*

> When you create stories or images in your mind, use your senses. Imagine how a German Shepherd smells, a strawberry tastes, the swirls in a bubble change in the air, or a teddy bear feels to a child. Pay attention to the world around you whenever you can. Run your hands across the rock patterns on a garden wall, breathe in as you walk through evergreen trees, or take a moment to notice the wax crayon colours in a child's drawing. The more details you imagine, the more you will remember.

Painting   *Colour*

Imagine bright colours when you create images in your mind. See the bright blue of a mountain stream, the dark green of pine needles, or the deep red of an autumn apple. Sometimes we think of things that are only in black and white or shades of grey. If you take your time you can make colours come alive. That is, unless you are colour blind. If that's the case, then this paragraph is really insensitive.

Whale   *Large*

Change the size of an object to make it more memorable in your mind. The movie *Journey 2: The Mysterious Island* features elephants the size of dogs and bees the size of horses. The change in size makes these creatures memorable. Changing the size also gives you the freedom to have any two things interact. You can imagine a mosquito surfing or a hippo threading a needle.

Fireworks   *Moving*

Move the objects in your mind. If things don't move they become a pile of junk. Think of how you notice a deer or a camouflaged hunter as soon as they start to move. Your mind will be attracted to the action of your stories. Think of your brain being a Tyrannosaurus Rex and the thing you want to remember being the annoying girl with the flashlight in *Jurassic Park*.

Camera   *Exciting*

Create stories like exciting parts of a movie. I love the final dance scene from *Footloose*, the melting metal scene from *Terminator*, and the lightsaber battle in *Star Wars* (Episodes IV, V, I, II, and VII). You can think of the stories in your mind being part of a movie directed by you. You can make anything happen.

Magician   *Magical*

Using magic with your images will make them memorable. Flowers that bloom from power drills, fish that can fly around a playground, or trees that can dance are things your mind will enjoy. Everybody loves magic. Well, everybody except Monique, my eleventh-grade crush. She said magic was childish, even though I made her necklace disappear. Her loss.

Teddy Bear   *Emotional*

Trigger emotions by imagining stories that make you giggle, cry, or turn up your nose. Anything that touches an emotion is going to be a memory. Imagine your favourite sweater getting wrecked by an oil spill, your crush giving you a donut dipped in a swamp, or your teacher using your toothbrush to wash her car. Keep it positive, though. There is already too much depression and anxiety in the world.

Lion   *Important*

Use things in your stories that are important. A rare blue diamond from Africa, your boss's Ferrari, or a cursed gold coin from pirate bounty are things you will remember more than a rock from your driveway, someone's white sedan, or a nickel from the kitchen drawer. Give the objects in your mind meaning and they will stay there longer.

Clown   *Humorous*

Make yourself laugh or smile with funny stories. Small accidents make me laugh. I laughed when my seven-year-old daughter hit a pothole and went flying over the handlebars of her dirt bike. I was still giggling when they X-rayed her left arm and ribs. I couldn't wait to tell the story to the dentist when he asked, "What happened to her teeth?" Fatherhood is fun.

Mirror   *Personal*

Remember that all of the images you make belong to you. Make them personal and your own style. You can create them however you want. No one else can see what you are thinking, so go crazy. Only your grandmother can see into your soul and she's not here right now.

brain magic

Logo designs

MEMORY CHALLENGE

For this challenge you will memorize company names and logos. Connecting abstract images to names is done by turning both pieces of information into a picture and then connecting them with a story.

Although the design of the logo may have other inspiration, it only matters what you see when you look at it. The BMW logo was designed to look like an airplane's propeller with blue parts for the sky and white parts for the clouds, but you might see something completely different when you look at it. You might see a pie with blueberry filling for the blue parts and whipped cream for the white parts. OK, maybe not. That was a lame idea.

Some logos will have the name of the company across it which will make it easier to remember. For ING Banking you could simply imagine a lion lying across three cement letters (I-N-G) to remember this logo.

For others you may have to imagine what the logo looks like. Maybe it reminds you of a vehicle, a building, a plant, an animal, or a toy. Whatever it looks like, use the image to create a story with the name.

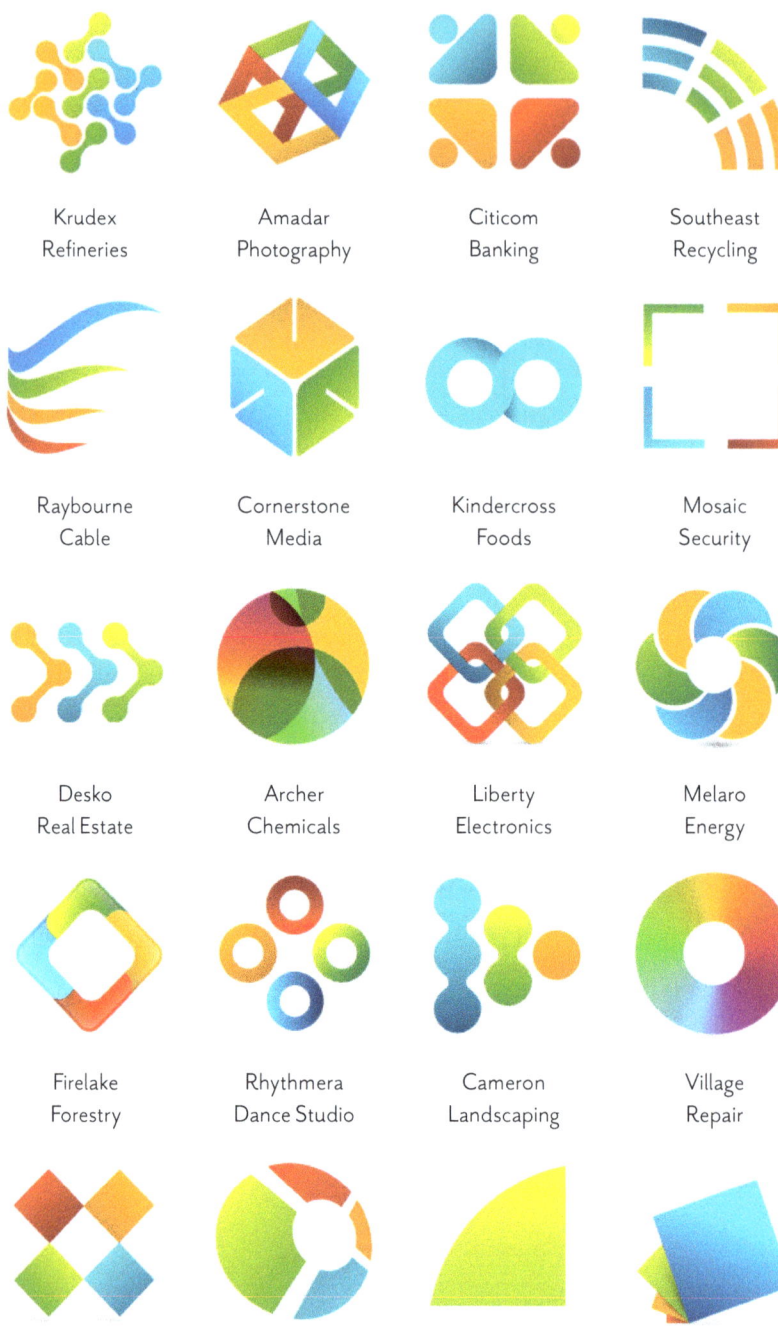

Logo designs

Cheat Sheet

Imagine:

- Atoms* are covered in crude oil (Krudex) floating above a refinery.
- A matador (Amadar) is taking pictures of a giant coloured cube*.
- Four men in triangular desks* are installing a city camera (Citicom) on a piggy bank.
- A Hawaiian with an Easter egg (Southeast) is placing empty bottles under a rainbow*.
- A sun in a cradle (Raybourne) is connected to a parrot* with a cable.
- A security guard is painting a mosaic on a Rubik's Cube*.
- Floating tubes* with food are going under a cross bridge made by kindergarten kids (Kindercross).
- A TV crew is putting stone in the corners (Cornerstone) of a cattle fence*.
- Three stealth jets* are shooting at a desk under a real estate sign.
- A woman in a chemical suit is shooting arrows (Archer) at a beach ball*.
- A mosquito with Malaria (Melaro) is taking a glowing globe of energy from the centre of a flower*.
- The Statue of (Liberty) is eating a frosted donut* while playing with her iPhone.

- A leaning television* is shooting out trees from a lake on fire (Firelake) scene.
- Four lifesavers candies* are playing rhythm drums (Rhythmera) for hula dancers.
- A bulldozer is pushing over bowling pins* with a camera on top (Cameron).
- The village people are installing a CD player* into a classic car.
- A cardboard box* full of mason jars (Masonair) is being shipped to a tropical island.
- A mad dozer (Amadeus) is shooting a canon at a spaceship*.
- A young lady is fanning* some tools off a marked grave (Gravemark).
- A carpenter is using a (Phillips) screwdriver to fasten pieces of paper* to Count Dracula.

it's Not cheating. Honest.

(Imagine playing ice hockey with skates and a stick, and everyone else is using snowshoes and pool noodles.)

Remembering things can become so easy, it'll seem unfair.

When I started using memory skills in the classroom, this was before there were official memory competitions. I had students who could memorize a list of 100 words in less than five minutes. This was not the idiot savant foreign exchange student who had just studied for four straight years in a monastery. These were average kids. And yes, there were more than one. About a third of the class could do this. I even had a girl who could memorize a deck of cards in five minutes, but at the time I didn't see the educational value in doing this. Plus she was too young to come to the casino with me, so it seemed pointless.

Now, since there were no competitions when I started (and I didn't know about these competitions even when they did start), it's impossible to know how these students would have fared. Later, in 2000, Chris Turner memorized 78 words in 15 minutes at the USA Memory Championship in New York.

Now trying to compare a fourth grader who can memorize 100 words in three minutes to an adult who could memorize 78 words in 15 minutes would not be easy. It would be like trying to decide who would win: LeBron James or Michael Jordan, Darth Vader or Voldemort, or (assuming the movie is just fiction) Batman vs. Superman. When two warriors are from completely different times, there are too many variables to really know who would win. There is no doubt, however, that these children were able to do something incredibly well before it was cool.

Today I am continuing to teach the memory skills as I have done for over 20 years with my students, but now I am including practicing for some of the events they have at memory competitions. If a child can memorize a list of words, it means that they can read the word, understand what it means, spell it correctly, and have an image that will come to mind the next time they read it. It also means that they will be able to do this with hundreds, even thousands, of words.

It also means that they are becoming very familiar with their memory palace. Each time they use one of the memory hooks, they visualize the details and see it from a different view. The storage places for information get stronger each time they use them.

Now that the students do this as part of learning in my classroom, it's easy to see how they compare to others. Results from competitions are posted online and some of the competitors share their stories about learning the memory skills. I have been doing this for so long that I have been able to fine-tune techniques, use shortcuts, and discover new strategies to remember information. My students are able to do amazing things, but they think it's routine.

Here are some highlights of learning:

> A five-year-old learned the times tables in a few hours using 'math stories'. Kids typically start learning multiplication in grade two or three, and most still can't do it by the time they are in grade six.
>
> His three-year-old little sister was listening to the same stories and could also repeat the stories, but had no idea what they meant.
>
> An entire class of third-graders learned the times tables in a few classes and most mastered them within a few weeks.
>
> A class of elementary students learned to play violin, guitar, and piano in four-part harmony, including chords, by Christmas of the school year (which starts in September).
>
> An eight-year-old learned to memorize a deck of cards in just a few weeks.
>
> A group of eleven-year-old students learned to memorize a list of 100 words that were in scrambled order in less than five minutes.

Since learning the academics of school became quick and easy, we were able to do much more in class. We built a picnic table to learn more about math concepts, performed plays such as versions of *Sherlock Holmes* and *Alice in Wonderland*, and created constructed hand-made chess sets to use in class. We performed music concerts, held math game tournaments, and made music videos of the school year. The memories of awesome things we did seem endless.

Because using memory skills have become a part of much of what I do with students in the classroom, I have been able to experiment with, discover, and improve ways of remembering. I know that the ways we do things are much faster. I'll try to explain one of the reasons with the memory palace.

The memory palace you learned in this book is something I have developed over several years. When one memory hook wasn't working, I changed it for another. It took some time, but eventually I had a complete memory palace from 0 to 100. This is something I have shared with my students. This may not seem like a big deal, but it does save a lot of time.

Most people have to create a palace. The time spent looking for unique objects that can be used as memory hooks may be lengthy. Whether you use rooms in a house or a path through a familiar place, you have to look for objects that can be used to make stories. You also have to put the objects in some kind of order to make them easy to find.

When you use the memory hooks and palaces here, then this work is already done for you. You can look at the images anytime you want instead of going to the rooms in your house or trails you know to strengthen the images in your mind. The hooks are organized, even colour-coded, so that they are easy to find. They are also palaces that you can share. Instead of everyone having different images, some better than others, everyone is working with the same set making it easy to learn from each other and share ideas. Imagine trying to learn how to fix a Mustang when the guy beside you is fixing a fridge. When things are the same, it makes it easier to work like a team.

I've also spent time making graphics to make it easy to visualize each memory palace and hook. We started out with just talking about the Kids Palace, then I drew (actually traced) pictures, then after a few other versions I created the posters you see in this book using computer graphic programs. Now I have these posters hanging up in the classroom, on the fridge, and on the bathroom wall. Hey, I don't judge the pictures you put up by the shower.

When an eight-year-old can learn to memorize a deck of cards in a few weeks (it would take an adult years to do the same), I know we are doing something right.

With great power comes great... um... greatness.

*(After Peter Parker got bit in the neck,
he still had to work at being Spiderman.)*

*Having a strong mind and memory
still takes a lot of work.*

Over time I developed ways of helping my students remember classroom stuff incredibly quickly. For example, normally it takes years of rote practice to master the times table, but I had grade three students learn the routines in a couple of hours and master them in just over a week. In fact, once you have learned to think with images and create stories to store information in places you can find later, you will have to practice to keep these skills up and get faster. You can think of the practice being similar to the way a track athlete trains. In fact, there are many similarities to these two types of 'training'.

A runner gets into a routine of running to increase cardiovascular fitness. This will increase the ability to run faster and longer. Practicing three to four times a week for 20 to 30 minutes will help you increase your memory skills. Think of this like jogging for your mind.

Runners often do different types of exercising or different forms of the same exercise. One athlete may swim on Thursday nights, take part in a drop-in fitness class at the recreation centre on Monday mornings, and play squash with some friends after work on Fridays. Another athlete may be dedicated to jogging, but she does a different jogging route every few days. Tuesdays are when she runs the long, paved trail through town. On Mondays and Thursdays she runs on the treadmill upstairs before she goes to work. On Fridays she runs a course with steep hills near her parents' farm.

Everybody has their own unique workout with different exercises, times, and goals. This is the same for memory training. Each person needs to find what works. A good place to start is to set some goals, start a routine, and adjust this as you find what is working and what is not.

A great way to practice memorizing is with a deck of cards. Since the ability to create images and stories is important for a good memory, memorizing the order of a deck of cards is an easy way to practice this. Using a stopwatch will let you see how much you improve over time. You can either see how quickly you can memorize an entire deck or see how many cards you can memorize in five minutes. Unless you are a little on the OCD side, and 'yes', I can relate, you may want to only practice for 20 to 30 minutes at a time. If you want to go longer, I can't really stop you. I'm not your mother.

Another great exercise is to memorize a list of 100 words. This not only improves your memory skills, but your vocabulary and spelling as well. If you search online you can find 'random word generators' that will give you lists to practice with. There are different levels of difficulty. For example, the United States format has simple, common words that are mainly nouns (that are easier to remember) and the international format that is similar to what is used at the World Memory Championships is much harder with all types of words.

Other sites offer other things you can practice such as names of people, both first and last; fictional historical dates; lists of numbers; and even poetry. All of these will help you develop your skills of remembering. As you repeat these skills, you will be able to visualize images more clearly, create better stories with less effort, and remember information more quickly. With enough work, these skills will become automatic - something you can do without thinking about it.

People want to know what a good score or time would be for memorizing. Though it will be different for each person, I can give you some guidelines. Every milestone should be celebrated, but I've set up some benchmarks to help you know how well you are doing with your memory skills.

If you are doing a skill for five minutes such as remembering a list of 100 words, then you can expect to reach certain benchmarks. I've included how you might feel if you were playing a sport. This works, since 'memory' is considered a sport by memory experts and officials. Just saying.

>20 If you can remember 20 words in five minutes, then be proud of yourself.
(You made the first round of tryouts.)

>30 You are more comfortable with the skills.
(You are on the short list and the coach is keeping her eye on you.)

>40 You are able to do these skills with ease.
(You're on the team.)

>50 You practice regularly.
(You are in the game.)

>55 You are doing these skills automatically.
(You are on the starting line-up.)

>65 You are feeling confident with your skills.
(You are now one of the team leaders.)

>70   You are now feeling competitive.
       (You are the team captain.)

>75   You are training hard.
       (You are on the all-star team.)

>85   You are becoming a master.
       (You are in the play-offs.)

>100   You are a master.
       (You are in the championship round.)

Once you are able to remember 100 words in five minutes, then it will take work to bring your time down even by a few seconds. Because it takes work to bring down your time or raise your score, it is important to keep track. At the back of the book there is a page for you to mark down your scores or times. Though there are benchmarks for each skill, you can put down your numbers whenever you want. Again, I'm not your mother.

If you want to compare your skills to the skills of other people, there are people who compete in competitions like the USA Memory Championships, Canadian Memory Championships, (other awesome country) Memory Championships, World Memory Championships, and even extreme competitions like Memoriad and the Extreme Memory Championships. There are competitions all over the world at all different levels. Many of these can be found online along with the rules, results, and records. Look at that. I aced alliteration and I wasn't even attempting.

You can join study groups, watch YouTube tutorials, or find other books on memory. If you are genuinely interested in memory skills, there is an entire subculture of memory enthusiasts - people who take the art of memory very seriously.

By definition, a genius is someone who displays exceptional intelligence or ability to acquire knowledge. Although only a small percentage of people can remember information at a high level, with these memory skills and practice, anyone can learn it.

i feel numb from numbers.

(I know, I know ...
It's like a never ending math class.)

Now that you have 100 mind shelves to put information,
you can use another system to remember other numbers.

The memory palaces you have built so far such as the 'Car Palace' and the 'Sports Palace' are great for putting information and can even double as numbers. The frog (with 16 toes) can be a place to put the 16th president of the United States (by imagining a frog with a Lincoln hat) or as a way to remember 16 as part of a phone number (such as a dentist having a pet frog that drives a car to remember the dentist's number is 1640).

Since there are so many numbers in our world, it would make sense that another way to remember numbers would give us the ability to remember more of them. Some people are able to remember long strings of numbers, as many as 50 to 100 in under 30 seconds (as Alex Mullen memorized 80 digits in 17.65 seconds in 2016 in the Extreme Memory Competition); or several hundred in five minutes (as Marwin Wallonius memorized 520 digits in five minutes in 2015 at the World Memory Competitions).

The Major System

One system that was created to remember numbers is the 'major system' which basically turns numbers into letters, letters into words, and words into pictures. For each number, there could be several letters that could be used since they sound similar. For example, since 6 looks like an upside-down g, a 6 can be a soft 'g' (like in gem) or any letter(s) that make a similar sound like ch (<u>ch</u>ain), sh (<u>sh</u>ack), or j (<u>j</u>uice).

Here is how the numbers are turned into letters:

Match	Reason	Other Letters
0 – z	(0 starts with 'z')	z, s, soft 'c'
1 - t	(1 downstroke)	t, d, th
2 - n	(2 downstrokes)	n
3 - m	(3 downstrokes)	m
4 - r	(4 looks like a backwards R)	r
5 - l	(50 in Roman Numerals is L)	l
6 - g	(6 looks like an upside-down g)	sh, ch, soft 'g', j
7 - k	(k looks like two 7s)	hard-g
8 - f	(8 if shaped like an 8)	f, v
9 - b	(9 looks like an upside-down b)	p, b

Typically letters are used in pairs. For example, an image to remember 32 is 'man'. Since the vowels don't change anything, the 'm' represents the digit

'3' and 'n' represents the digit '2'. To become familiar with all the images you could use, you will have to memorize 100 images from 00 to 99.

Other images for two-digit numbers could be:

91	bat	45	rail	36	mug
83	foam	72	cane	90	booze
27	knife	56	log	31	mutt

Some memory athletes who enter competitions often use one image for three digits. For example, 'bison' could be an image for '902' (b for 9, s for 0, and n for 2). To become familiar with all the images you could use, you will have to memorize 1000 images from 000 to 999.

Images for two-digit numbers could be:

235-(nml)-animal	792-(kbn)-cabin	148-(trf)-trophy
650-(jlz)-Julius	825-(fnl)-funnel	914-(btr)-batter
084-(zfr)-sapphire	752-(kln)-cologne	461-(rbt)-rabbit

Some athletes have gone through the work of finding an image for four-digit images. Simon Reinhart from Germany is one who has claimed to have created and memorized a system of 10,000 images using letters instead of numbers, and from his scores and world memory titles, I believe him.

I have adapted the major system slightly to a system that is faster and easier for kids to learn.

Each digit, 0 through 9, matches up with only one sound.

0-C   (0 looks like a C.)

1-L   (1 looks like a 1.)

2-N   (2 looks like a sideways N.)

3-M   (3 looks like an sideways M.)

4-R   (4 looks like a backwards R.)

5-S   (5 looks like an S.)

6-B   (6 looks like a b.)

7-V   (7 looks like a sideways V.)

8-G   (8 looks like a g.)

9-J   (9 looks like a J.)

This narrows down the possibilities. With the major system, the number '66' could be 'shush', 'church', 'judge', 'josh', or other possibilities. However if we only use 'b' and often use a common vowel sound 'a', then the only logical image is 'baby'. I also made this system so I could use the other letters for memorizing binary numbers (strings of 0s and 1s like 011010010110101111010…). I know it seems weird, but memory competitions have events to memorize these numbers too. It's like they look for impossible things to remember. I'm surprised 'product barcodes' isn't an event. Here are the two-digit images I use. Though you will come up with your own images, these may give you some ideas.

00	(cc)	cook (*Ratatouille*)	10	(lc)	Luke (Skywalker)
01	(cl)	coal (miner)	11	(ll)	Lil' John
02	(cn)	kong (KIng Kong)	12	(ln)	loner (wolf)
03	(cm)	cameraman	13	(lm)	lime (*Shrek*)
04	(cr)	karate (*Karate Kid*)	14	(lr)	Laura (Croft)
05	(cs)	case (farmer)	15	(ls)	Elsa (from *Frozen*)
06	(cb)	Qbert	16	(lb)	lab (Beeker)
07	(cv)	cave (caveman)	17	(lv)	love (tennis player)
08	(cg)	cog (mechanic)	18	(lg)	log (log roller)
09	(cj)	cage (Tweety)	19	(lj)	lodge (member)
20	(nc)	nuke (Homer)	30	(mc)	Mike (Wazowski)
21	(nl)	nail (carpenter)	31	(ml)	mailman
22	(nn)	nanny	32	(mn)	moon (astronaut)
23	(nm)	Nemo	33	(mm)	mummy
24	(nr)	north (elf)	34	(mr)	Mario
25	(ns)	Elsa (from *Frozen*)	35	(ms)	moose
26	(nb)	Newbie	36	(mb)	Moby (whale)
27	(nv)	November (war vet)	37	(mv)	movie (Spielberg)
28	(ng)	nugget (goldminer)	38	(mg)	Magneto
29	(nj)	ninja (turtle)	39	(mj)	magician

40	(rc)	rock (The Rock)	50	(sc)	seeker (Harry)
41	(rl)	Ariel	51	(sl)	Sulley
42	(rn)	iron (ironman)	52	(sn)	sand (Sandman)
43	(rm)	ram	53	(sm)	sumo wrestler
44	(rr)	rare (bird)	54	(sr)	sorcerer
45	(rs)	race (Armstrong)	55	(ss)	sister (nun)
46	(rb)	rabbit	56	(sb)	saber (tiger)
47	(rv)	raven	57	(sv)	saviour
48	(rg)	rug (Aladdin)	58	(sg)	soggy (mudder)
49	(rj)	rage (Anger)	59	(sj)	sage

60	(bc)	baker	70	(vc)	Viking
61	(bl)	Belle (& the Beast)	71	(vl)	Violet
62	(bn)	Bane	72	(vn)	Venus
63	(bm)	beam (Scotty)	73	(vm)	vampire
64	(br)	bear	74	(vr)	veer (Vector)
65	(bs)	bass (guitar player)	75	(vs)	vase (sculptor)
66	(bb)	baby	76	(vv)	vibe (musician)
67	(bv)	above (angel)	77	(vv)	valve (plumber)
68	(bg)	bug (Flick)	78	(vg)	Vogue (Madonna)
69	(bj)	badge (officer)	79	(vj)	veg (gardener)

80	(gc)	gecko		90	(jc)	Jake (Avatar)
81	(gl)	goal (Crosby)		91	(jl)	jail (prisoner)
82	(gn)	goon		92	(jn)	Jane (Tarzan)
83	(gm)	game (Ralph)		93	(jm)	Jim (Carrey)
84	(gr)	gear (climber)		94	(jr)	jar (Grandma)
85	(gs)	ghost (Casper)		95	(js)	Jess (*Toy Story*)
86	(gg)	Gabe (statue)		96	(jj)	jab (Bruce Lee)
87	(gv)	give (Santa		97	(jv)	jive (Potsy)
88	(gg)	Gaga		98	(jg)	jug (milkman)
89	(gj)	Gadget (Inspector)		99	(jj)	judge (Judy)

(If you don't know who these 'people' are, just Google them.)

At memory competitions such as the World Memory Championships, one of the events is memorizing numbers. Competitors are asked to memorize strings of numbers in a set amount of time. Numbers are in a grid with rows of 20, 30, or 40 digits and can be one, five, or 15 minutes - or even 60 minutes.

Competitors have come up with different strategies for memorizing numbers that basically connect smaller strings of numbers together so they can be put into a memory palace. One of the more common ways to do this is to use the PAO method.

PAO Method

The PAO method connects three objects (often from two-digit words) to form one image in a specific place in your mind. 'P' stands for *'Person'*, 'A' stands for *'Action'*, and 'O' stands for *'object'*. For every object you are going to have a **person** doing an **action** to an **object**. This is sounding like a lecture, so before I put myself to sleep, why don't I just give you an example.

(21) | 7 | 3 | 6 | 6 | 4 | 5 | 7 | 0 | 5 | 5 | 4 | 2 | 3 | 4 | 6 | 6 | 4 | 5 | 7 | 1 |

Here is a row with 20 digits, something you might see in a memory competition. Though practicing memorizing strings of numbers seems ~~inpractical~~ ~~unpractical~~ ~~practicalnessless~~ not useful, you can use the same technique for memorizing phone numbers, passwords, or credit card numbers. Make sure you only memorize your own credit card numbers. Apparently it's a big deal with the authorities and federal agents. I had to find that out the hard way.

To memorize the first six digits (746690), imagine a *vampire* (a person for 73) squirting a *baby* bottle (an action for 66) at a *rac*ing bike (an object for 45). This one image will help you remember six digits. You put this image in one of your memory palaces. For example, you could imagine a vampire squirting a baby bottle over a racing bike near the fire hydrant (the 21st place in the Mega-Palace since it's the 21st row).

You may find that only using a person and an object (such as a vampire squirting a baby bottle) will work faster for you. Making a longer string (such as a vampire squirting a bike into a Viking ship) will allow you to remember more numbers. The great thing about memorizing is that it is up to you how you want to remember and what you are going to do with all the money from credit cards. Sorry, I didn't mean to say that out loud. Obey the law… and be kind to your mother.

Mad Math Skills

I teach math at an elementary school and early on I found that most kids don't know the basics. By the time they are 11 or 12 years old, they should know how to add, subtract, multiply, and divide. Most, however, don't. Only about one third know these 'basic facts' well enough to do well in math. The rest struggle (having to resort to counting fingers or lines on a worksheet) or don't know them at all.

If you want to know if a child struggles with math, ask them what 6 x 7 is. It should only take a student three seconds to answer. If it takes them any longer, especially if they have to count fingers, then they are going to be behind in math. Sometimes I have to wait 30 seconds or longer for a child to come up with an answer. Imagine a construction worker counting on his fingers while his boss patiently waits for him to count out supplies using his fingers... and toes. You'd be surprised how many workers can't count to twenty-one unless they're naked.

Seeing kids struggle with numbers in class is often painful. They look up... then down... then up again... then at you... then down again. Sometimes they look constipated. Other times they look like they smell a skunk. Oftentimes they ask to go to the bathroom just to leave the situation, all the while breathing like someone dropped an ice-cube between their cheeks.

I have taught many of these children to use memory skills to master basic math skills. What they couldn't master after years of counting sets, skip counting, or doing worksheets, they were able to master in a few short days or weeks with simple images. As not everyone is ready to imagine weird and crazy stories, I started with simple, easy-to-remember phrases. Here is an example of the images I use to teach the times tables.

Most people don't realize how difficult it is for children to learn the times tables. For many children it takes years and they are still only able to count by 2's, 5's, and maybe by 9's if they learn the creepy finger trick. With this method, they still need to put in work, but it takes only a fraction of the time that it takes to learn traditional methods. I can already feel the old-school teacher rolling their eyes.

Basically a child is learning to connect two words: one for the two numbers in the question, and one for answer. The word 'giggles' would be for the two 8's in the question (8 x 8) and 'bear' would be for the answer (64). These words are connected with the sentence 'She giggles with her bear.'

As you have read through this book you have realized that effective ways of remembering are not traditional. This is no different. In a class of 10 and 11 year olds I measured their ability to answer basic multiplication questions. Two weeks after starting school, students were able to answer on average eight questions in five minutes. After using this method for one month, these same students were able to answer 120 questions in the same amount of time. You'd think that more teachers would be excited to learn these strategies.

i felt like i was raised by wolves.

(Even though these methods work incredibly well, not everyone is ready to do things differently.)

A child in my math class was finally succeeding in math, but his mother was upset that he used the name 'Moby'.

I started working on memory skills my first year of college, which was over 25 years ago. Since then I have realized that not everyone is ready to try these strategies. It seems people will find any reason to discredit the methods, even when the results are clear.

I taught guitar, piano, and violin as part of my music class. Many of the children had never touched these instruments before. One boy with a few 'learning disabilities' was able to master the melodies and harmonies of several songs after only a few weeks of practice with an acoustic guitar. His mother picked him up from school one day and heard me talking to him. She asked about his music and instead of telling her, I thought I'd let this young man show her. He played a song I had composed for the class perfectly, which is tough to do on the spot. His mother's only reaction was one of disappointment that he was not using a pick, the small piece of plastic for plucking the strings. Although he had learned to play with or without a pick in class, I didn't really feel like explaining this.

As I use memory skills in math, language arts, and music, I have found many ways to make learning and remembering easier. Until last year, however, I felt like I was doing this alone. No other teachers used these methods, parents were not familiar with mnemonics, and administration did not support non-traditional teaching methods I often felt like I was alone in the wild, being raised by wolves.

Now I realize that more people were using these methods, just not anyone I knew. Around the time I started using memory techniques in class, the World Memory Championships started where people could compete in events like cards, names, numbers, and even poetry. I wasn't given a phone call, letter, email, or even text. Nothing. My feelings are still hurt.

I did eventually find out about these competitions and am now a fan... and a competitor. At first I thought that at my age I was too old to compete, especially since scores have steadily increased and now seem superhuman. I am, however, now giving it a shot. My hope is that the more I learn from these competitions, the more I'll be able to share in the classroom. After training for a little over a year, I am now able to keep up with the 'big dogs' of memory. Keep in mind, this is relative. The fastest competitor in the world can memorize a deck of cards in under 20 seconds, others have won national titles for doing this in less than two minutes, while others have won state titles for remembering more than 20 cards in five minutes. I would never win the title in England, but I am pretty sure I could place top five at the Corn Valley County Fair, if there was such a place and they had a memory competition. I guess a better way to give you an idea of how I've done is to show you my score. For example, I have reached the top 20 in the Memory League ranking, an online memory competition. Here is my biased opinion on how I have performed in four of the events:

Names:

I have memorized 30 names in one minute. After looking at the faces of random people with common first names for one minute, I was able to remember names such as Ashley, Julia, Kevin, Christopher, and Catherine. This is harder than it sounds, since spelling counts. If you write down Kara instead of Kari, Bryan instead of Brian, Kathy instead of Kate, or Steven instead of Stephen then you don't get the points. The first time all 30 names were memorized in one minute in competition was in 2016 by Katie Kermode. Though I haven't officially competed in this event, I did get this perfect score while sitting on the couch wearing mismatched socks watching *Captain America: Civil War* and eating Doritos. Sure, Katie was able to do it with the pressure of competition and thousands of dollars on the line, but I did it during the fight scene between Iron Man and Captain America. *(drops the mic...)*

Cards:

I competed in this event at our provincial and national memory competitions but didn't perform well under pressure. I thought I had memorized the entire deck in under two minutes, but three of my four attempts were flawed by two switched cards. On my best attempt I made sure I didn't make any mistakes and memorized one deck in five minutes, which is about the same as my daughter's score. My latest attempt was scheduled for March 31 but I ended up in the hospital from complications from my third brain surgery a month earlier. I still did an unofficial attempt in the hospital and memorized a deck in 1:14. Now I am able to remember the correct order of a full deck in about 60 seconds consistently, and I am still improving. When I am at home in the comfort of my own living room in my own cowboy pyjamas I can memorize a deck in scrambled order. This means that each card has a random number attached to it. For example, the first card has the number 37 on it, the second card has the number 18 on it, the third card has the number 29 on it, and so on. After flipping through these scrambled cards for two minutes, I can recall them in order. I mainly use this skill to win at Crazy Eights with my kids.

Numbers:

Being a math person, this probably should be my best event, but I'll admit the other events like *Names* and *Images* are a little more fun for me. I am able to remember a string of 60 numbers in 60 seconds. I guess I could have said I can memorize a number every second, but that doesn't sound as cool. What's ironic about this is that I still have to ask my wife for our land address or our Visa card number. I know what you're thinking: sharing a credit card is very romantic.

Images:

There is a very cool event that Simon Orton created for an online memory competition. Essentially it measures how quickly you can memorize the order of random pictures. Pictures may be of animals, buildings, people, landmarks, or vehicles. I am able to memorize the order of 30 images in about 20 seconds. After 20 seconds of studying I can tell you that an evergreen tree was the fifth picture, a mother duck with five ducklings was the 13th picture, and a pattern of clouds was the second picture. My relatives are very impressed at holiday gatherings. Actually, they all think I watch too much TV.

Some other life achievements I think are pretty important include getting fourth place out of five entries in a science fair in fifth grade. I also got a purple ribbon in shot-put at our county track and field day. My second grade teacher gave me a gold sticker for a clay sculpture of the Flintstone's car. I think I can hold my own when it comes to achieving.

I held small competitions in my class years ago, but nothing like the competitions that exist today. There are events for memorizing cards, names, dates, poems, numbers, images, and even binary numbers (strings of numbers made up of only 1's and 0's). Each event has different levels and variations. For example, Names for the Memory League asks you to memorize simple first names for one minute and the World Memory Championships has you memorize complex first and last names for 15 minutes. Most competitions have Speed Cards to see how quickly a deck can be memorized, but some competitions see how many cards/decks can be memorized in an hour. An hour! That's 60 minutes of memorizing. I'm lucky if I can watch a Super Bowl commercial through to the end.

Each year these competitions continue to grow with larger prize money, more refined strategies, and more participants. As the sport becomes more popular, it seems that the scores get better and better. For example, in 2000 the United States record for memorizing cards was 22 cards in five minutes. In 2016 it was 52 cards in 18.65 seconds. Some countries have annual competitions while others are still catching up. Canada's memory sport is growing; we just have to stop building igloos, playing hockey, riding caribou, chopping down trees, eating donuts, and apologizing for a few weeks to train.

i bet i'm less competitive than you.

My dad tricked me into exercising by saying "Race you to the car!" or "Last one to the kitchen table gets hypothermia!"

Just like training for a triathlon makes you a better athlete, training for a memory competition makes you a better thinker.

The first competition that I entered was one that I helped organize: our provincials in March 2016. Most of the competitors were students from my class who had learned the memory skills to memorize cards. There were 21 students plus myself with a group of parents led by a good friend of mine acting as arbitrators. It was our first time with the event so we were fumbling through, trying to make it as official as possible. As much as we tried, things still went wrong. The rules said the competition was to be held in a 'public venue' so I chose the library of the elementary school. The library was in the centre of a pod of grade one and two classrooms, so I waited until just after lunch break when I thought it would be the quietest.

Thirty seconds into the memorization period the secretary came on the intercom and blah blah blahhed an announcement about teachers not taking attendance. A few seconds later the kindergarten class began a stomping and chanting game and a program assistant started tearing paper boxes for the recycling bin. Just before we finished, a maintenance crew wandered in and began discussing light fixtures very loudly at the front of the library. I couldn't believe how many distractions there were for my class.

During the recall period I got halfway through sorting my cards when my friend, Stephen, told me to stop. Just me. I said, "No, I still have more time." We began arguing like four-year-olds, when I realized my class was watching. So I complied, sat down, and pouted. He then came over and told me he was 'just kidding'. I didn't know what to do as I had lost my train of thought, but I put the two cards in my hand down (in the wrong order) and ordered the rest of the deck. We laugh about it now, but I switched two cards when he stopped me and lost the title of provincial champion to two ten-year-olds. I don't think we could have fit more mishaps into a ten-minute span if we tried.

Even though my first experience was less than perfect, I wanted to keep trying. I also wanted to learn from people who were serious memory athletes. Katie Kermode is one who has competed in national and world memory competitions. She has won titles and currently holds the world record for Names and Words. I have been asking her to help me with some pointers as I plan on taking part in more official events. I also want to keep helping people who wish to learn more about memory, especially those who are thinking about competing. So, with Katie's help, here are some suggestions for doing well in the sport of memory:

Know your palaces well.

Since you will be using your palaces over and over, you should know them well. Know every detail and practice them as much as you can. You can add more to each palace if you think it will help you remember, such as a person. The number 2 place on the Mega-Palace is a dolphin but you can imagine the theme park, dolphin trainer, and audience as part of this palace. These palaces will be with you forever, becoming part of your soul and very being. Ok, maybe that's a little far. I got carried away in the moment.

Have a database of objects.

Choose an object for everything you might come across on a regular basis. If you are studying cards, you should have an object for every card in the deck, and probably a person and action to go with it. You should have a standard object for common names. It is easy to find lists of common first names and surnames. You should have an object for every number from 00-99 no matter what system you use. Whatever you are studying, you should have a bank of images to draw from. Use objects that work for you. I use a *yacht* for the name *Cathy* because they both have the same letters.

Learn to exercise your mind.

Your mind is like a muscle in many ways and it is okay to treat it like one. If you are practicing cards, you can practice in sets the same way a weightlifter would at the gym. Practice for 60 seconds, and then take a 30-second rest. Repeat this sequence at least four times. When you get stronger, you can increase the amount of time you practice or the number of repetitions you do. You can isolate skills like isolating muscles in the gym. Practice only remembering the images for each card without putting them into a palace. You can practice before work or school, when you get home, or before you go to bed. Find a routine for training, a quiet place to work, and a way to track your progress. You could also get a cool headband with a graphic of a butterfly, leather gloves, and sports bra just so you look like a real memory athlete. Speaking from experience, just know they might not let you into the grocery store when you wear these things.

Be creative with your objects.

Using the memory objects in this book will work, but you can always create your own. When memorizing cards, you can remember the king of clubs as a character from *Game of Thrones, The Flintstones,* or the NFL. In fact, you can use the Flintstones for all the clubs. Maybe Wilma is the queen of clubs, Barney is the jack of clubs, and Pebbles is the two of clubs. If you are into sports, each number or suit could be from a certain team or sport. Maybe all of the fours are from soccer. If you are into video games, maybe all of the hearts are from Pokémon and your palaces are from Minecraft. If you are a music buff, then maybe all of the nines are from country music. Each person is going to have a different idea for objects. When remembering birthdays, one person might have a box of chocolate from Valentine's Day, another person might have a cage from Groundhog Day, and another person might have a cloud from National Weatherman's Day. Our creative differences are what make us brilliant, or in my case, 'subject to psychological assessment'.

Teach others.

When I learned First Aid, I learned enough that I could keep someone alive until help arrived. When I had to teach it, I went back and researched specifics about treatment, put checklists into easy to remember mnemonics, and perfected my treatment steps so I could demonstrate for the class. When I teach math stories to elementary students, I often get them to teach a younger 'buddy' class to reinforce the skills. Anyone who has had to teach a class knows how much more focused you are when you know you are going to have an audience.

Memory skills do not have to be taught like a university course. It can be as simple as teaching someone the notes on sheet music using pictures, teaching a group of simple stories to remember each other's names, or a making a story to chain together the notes for a unit in science. The people who compete will all tell you the same thing: anyone can do well. People love to share their ideas. It doesn't mean that everyone will do well, but they could if they practiced. I compete so that I can help others learn. I like to play guitar, but I love to sit beside someone who is learning harmonies for the first time. I like looking for patterns in numbers and solving the tough questions, but I love watching the light go on for someone else who suddenly sees numbers differently. I had my taste of fame when I won a 12-pack of Pepsi from the local television station. Sure, they made me pay the deposit, but they put my name on the screen in red at the end of the show. You could say I've been kind of a celebrity since then, but I still love working with those who want to learn - especially the little people (children).

brain magic trivia

The butterfly was chosen as a symbol for **Brain Magic** because it symbolizes 'change'. In order to develop a brilliant mind, change must take place. You must shed the old, traditional methods of rote memorization and teaching children like they are factory workers that need to be trained. The butterfly is also one of the main images for music (to remember such things as the 'b' note and notes in 'B' chords), numbers (since it's the number 34 in the mega-palace), and letters to remember the shape of upper and lower case b's. I love butterflies. And ice cream.

The colours for the memory palaces come from the game of pool (8-ball). The number 1 pool ball is yellow (as is every number 1 in the palaces such as the banana, fire hydrant, and baseball bat). The number 2 ball is blue (just like the number 2's on each list like the dolphin, globe, and blue jay). The number 3-ball is red (like the tricycle), the 4-ball is purple (like the kite), the 5-ball is orange (like the boxing gloves), and so on. Obviously the 8-ball is black. The metal rack for the 9-ball is grey, and the 10th ball on the table (the cue ball) is white. This seems to be a colour pattern that could work with number connections, so I built the palaces based on these colours.

When recording a video of my son doing his times tables when he was five, my daughter couldn't keep quiet because she was reciting the answers in the background. It took me a while to figure out what the sound was. She was supposed to be colouring, but she was listening instead, and she was saying the answers like a cute little parrot. She was able to recite all of the 'math stories' I use to teach the times tables. She was two years old, turning three in a few months. I was going to say she was 31 months old, but when I do that it just sounds weird. I told someone I was four hundred and twenty-eight months old and she just stared at me like I had just killed her goldfish and was waiting for an apology. Weird.

Over 15 years ago I taught several students who could memorize a list of 100 words in less than five minutes, some of them under three minutes. This was before memory competitions were popular. They would have easily broken the national records (had we known about them), even breaking the ones that exist today. These students could also memorize them out-of-order. This seems like an impossible task, but now that I have learned about memory competitions, I have students who have learned the skills and are now capable of the same.

When I first learned about memory, I was working as a lifeguard at Mill Creek Pool, an outdoor pool in the heart of Edmonton. The manager gave me a gift certificate to Earls (a local restaurant) to give away. I told the kids from school groups at the pool that if I forgot anyone's name, they would get the prize. As they jumped in the water one by one I asked their name and then took a few seconds to lock it into my memory. Of the roughly 400 students there, I didn't have to give away the gift certificate to anyone. GO TEAM!

The first memory books I looked at included some 'adult' themes like ex-say, iolence-vay, and ain-pay. Sorry, my Pig Latin is a little rusty, but you get the idea. I found using these dark ways to remember things just didn't feel right, especially in an elementary school setting. They would later be popular during Harry Potter and Game of Thrones book club meetings, however. I found that these images weren't ones I wanted to use to teach children memory techniques. However, if they work for you, we don't judge.

Other names we considered for this book are *Mind Games*, *The Learning Tree*, *The Brick School* (referring to old school methods of learning), *Brain Magic*, *Change your Mind*, and *The Green School* (referring to how this learning is organic and grows with time). My grandmother didn't get it, so we moved on. To be honest, we still haven't settled on a title.

Since I have been working with memory for so long, I've come up with ways to remember, among other things, concepts in math, language arts, and music. I've shared some of them in this book, but there are too many strategies to put inside just one book. I've put together other books that go through methods for teaching such math skills as addition and multiplication and concepts like geometry, fractions, and algebra. I realize this looks like self-promotion, which it totally is, but I want to make sure people know that these materials are available (on our website: brainmagic.ca). If you have a child who is struggling with math or having trouble reading, at least you know that there are other options. If you have trouble finding the time or money to invest in lessons but you still want your child to have the gift of music, there are ways to make that happen.

We have created ~~a bunch~~... ~~a plethora~~ ... ~~a gaggle~~...a lot of board games for learning and we have hidden seven butterflies in each one. These games are just one more way to keep the mind active... and offer more self-promotion. We might have done the same thing on the cover of this book. I'm not really sure as we are still working on the cover. We took inspiration from Jerry Seinfeld who hid a Superman somewhere in most of the episodes of his show. I'm not sure if anyone notices, but my grandmother thinks it's cool. I thought about hiding a map to pirate treasure in the images inside the book, but I can't make maps and I don't have any treasure. Not to mention I'm not twelve years old.

I really hope you have enjoyed this book. It started off as something I did for my family and now it is something I have been able to share with many people, some of whom I have never met. I thank you most sincerely for taking the time to read my book. I hope you make great memories with it.

Many people believe that only a few can have a brilliant mind. I hope this book has changed your mind.

Darren Mark Michalczuk

More Memory Challenges

Here are some other things you can memorize. You can check them off if you want, but you may want to save this book for a friend. Nothing says 'Happy Birthday' better than a used book about learning.

- [ ] characters from the Harry Potter books
- [ ] the Presidents of the United States
- [ ] a 16-line poem
- [ ] names from a yearbook page
- [ ] countries in South America
- [ ] Super Bowl champions
- [ ] licence plates of vehicles in a parking lot
- [ ] Spanish vocabulary words
- [ ] digits of Pi
- [ ] chapter titles in *The Hobbit*
- [ ] headlines in a newspaper
- [ ] Academy Award-winning movies
- [ ] Stanley Cup winners
- [ ] Canadian prime ministers
- [ ] hockey team roster
- [ ] songs on a CD
- [ ] years for major inventions
- [ ] coordinates of Area 51

biography

Darren Michalczuk, a teacher for over twenty years, has taught everything from kindergarten to grade nine. Being a homeroom teacher for all grades, a physical education and music specialist, and an education consultant has given him the opportunity to work with thousands of students including hundreds of special needs children.

Darren is passionate about learning. He has written and directed over twenty plays including versions of *Sherlock Holmes*, *Robin Hood*, and *The Wizard of Oz* complete with songs, costumes, and sets.

Along with coaching many sports from little league soccer to recreation hockey to girls' varsity volleyball, he has organized many events including dances, tournaments, and triathlons. Introducing many higher level learning activities into the classroom such as cooking and carpentry is another trademark of his teaching style.

As part of his education career Darren has:

- spoken at events including Literary Conferences;
- appeared on *Dragons' Den* with educational resources;
- developed and designed apps for Apple;
- designed games which were sold at Indigo Chapters; and
- authored a book entitled *The Perfect School*.

He has facilitated Professional Development for such schools as:

- Sturgeon School Division   Ochre Park School
- Aspen View School Division   Landing Trail School
- Living Sky School Division   Unity School
- Black Gold School Division Corinthia Park School

Most recently he has presented at Teachers' Conventions such as:

- 2015 BC Christian Teachers' Convention
- 2015 Palliser Teachers' Convention
- 2015 Mighty Peace Teachers' Convention
- 2015 Greater Edmonton North Teachers' Convention

As a father he is proud of the fact that he has taught his children to swim, ski, dirt bike, and play music. He has organized Daddy/Daughter Balls, triathlons, and outside movie nights as excuses to hang out with his children. He has built treehouses, skating rinks, and outdoor furniture like picnic tables where he and Mac, Kieran, Noah, and his beautiful wife, Tanya, have shared many memories together. He spends every minute he can with his family, whether he's helping them with homework, listening to stories about their day, or explaining the changes that come with growing up. He works really hard to be a great father.

Darren is a passionate teacher, developer, and father of three. He will captivate you with his humour, intelligence, creativity, and ability to make learning fun, fast, and easy for anyone.

My son, Noah, and my daughter, Mackenzie, tied for first place at the Canadian Memory Championships. Though there haven't been any kids before them, kids have tried and have yet to beat Mackenzie's card memorizing score.

This is a picture of one of my students doing math. I had a group of kids that really struggled with math, but after doing things differently, they were able to do work that was well above grade level. You can see how hard the questions are.

This is my son Kieran. I have pics of my other two kids, so I thought I'd include this one. This is him skiing at Tawatinaw Valley. It's just a really cool pic.

My daughter did her provincial competition trial in my hospital room (as I was recovering from brain surgery complications). Without any practice she was able to memorize 29 cards (officially the best in Canada for the kids category) in five minutes perfectly. I memorized a deck in a minute and 14 seconds, which would have been the fastest in Canada so far, but it wasn't official because none of the nurses wanted to be a judge. They were too busy "checking my vitals".

Darren Mark Michalczuk

www.ingramcontent.com/pod-product-compliance
Lightning Source LLC
Chambersburg PA
CBHW040422100526
44589CB00022B/2802